Happy and Healed

Five Steps to
Getting over ANY Man and
Finding the Love You Deserve

Lady Shepsa Jones

Happy and Healed

Five Steps to
Getting over ANY Man and
Finding the Love You Deserve

Copyright © 2015 by Tameka Jones

ISBN: 978-0692474440 (Let Go Let Goddess)

Dedication

Ore Yeye O! Oshun Iyalode!

Thank you, Oshun, for leading me on this path to happiness, healing, and wholeness.

May we all receive and *be* the love we deserve.

Contents

Introduction

Do you want to be happy, *really* happy? So happy that your body seems to burst with joy? Are you ready to be healed, for your heart and mind to be bathed in peace and made whole? Do you want to let go of that man who is no good for you? Is it time for you to attract the REAL love you deserve?

There are a lot of books that tell you how to get a man. "Think like a man" gurus promise to teach you how to make any man "fall head over heels for you," and even how to make a man text you back! These people are marketing to a perceived weakness in women, the idea that most of us have our happiness hinged on a relationship or being able to "snag" a man.

I am not that guru. I make no such promises. My goal is not for you to find a man, but for you to find yourself, to heal yourself and become such a powerhouse of self-love that WHATEVER you desire comes to you at the perfect place and the perfect time. No begging or manipulation required.

This is goddess work.

This work is not for women who want to play victim or for women who are willing to stay addicted to the same cycles and patterns that are keeping them trapped in unfulfilling lives and relationships. This is for women who are ready for an inner revolution and an outer expansion into a life full of happiness.

If you're looking for games, tricks, or makeup tips, you've come to the wrong place. But, if you want to release the past so you can step into a dynamic NOW, welcome. If you want to open the wellspring of JOY within you, which is INDEPENDENT of anyone else or outer circumstances, welcome. If you desire to turn on your juicy, magnetic feminine energy, bienvenidos!

This is also not a book against men. I absolutely love men, so, this will not be a book where I beat down men and frame them as "no good dogs." It's time for a different conversation.

I have grown weary of hearing and seeing repeated cycles of trauma and drama with women who have no clue why their life is the way it is, and who think it's because of everyone except themselves. Letting go of someone can be tough, but what you receive instead is something money cannot buy—your dignity and real happiness.

So, welcome aboard for this luscious journey! When we finish, you will be so full of power, peace, and pleasure that whoever "he" is will be a distant memory and far from your mind. You will be open to a beautiful NOW, full of passion and more joy than you can imagine!

I know, because I have walked this path. These are the tools I have used, time and again, to pull me out of heartbreak after heartbreak. You see, I have been where many of you are. Maybe in different shades and hues, but with the same end result—having to pick myself up again after *another* disappointment.

Clutching my chest as I shattered into tears, because I couldn't believe *he* did this to *me*. Having visions of slashing car tires, breaking glasses, and "busting windows" out of cars; or even worse, doubting my own beauty and power as a woman and a lover.

But there is a better way. There is a way to rise, like a glorious sexy phoenix out of the ashes of any break-up, and I am here to show you how.

My Story . . .

When I was 27, I found myself separated from my now ex-husband and braving the dating world as a single mother. Making the decision to leave my marriage, when I had a two-year-old son, was absolutely the hardest thing I ever did in my life.

I had to do a tremendous amount of healing work to support that decision and, honestly, it was one of the best decisions I ever made. But, it did not feel like it at the time. It felt like pure hell.

Although I knew my ex was a good man, I knew he was not the man for *me*. As a matter of fact, I had never truly investigated what I wanted in a man. I found myself almost 30 and on the dating scene for the first time—yes, the first time!

I had only dated and had sex with one man—my husband. My background had a lot to do with this. I grew up in the rough inner city of Philadelphia and found my solace in books and writing. I was a nerd, the goodie-goodie girl who everyone wanted to cheat off of in middle school. For me, academics and the arts were my ticket out of the 'hood.

I quickly learned that my mind and my way with words gave me a cushion from some of the harsh realities of my environment. My mother was a single mother, raising three children while working fulltime and going to school. My father was a drug addict until I was the age of 11. I remember my best friend from fifth grade getting pregnant by the time she was in eighth grade. So, for me, doing well in school and staying away from boys meant staying out of trouble and not repeating the cycle of despair I witnessed around me.

Well, it worked. By the time I was 18, I was a consistent honor student, graduating from one of the top high schools in Philadelphia and the winner of many local and national awards for my creative writing. I was chosen by Scholastic Press to give a speech at the White House. I shook President Bill Clinton's hand as one of only 20 national Presidential Scholars in the Arts. I even had my face painted on the largest mural on the east coast, the Common Threads mural, on Broad and Spring Garden Street in Philadelphia. (It's still there! Google me, baby!)

I got accepted into my first-choice college, New York University (NYU), as a drama major. The summer before I went to college, I went to Africa for the first time to perform and engage in cultural exchanges. It was a whirlwind of achievement that was enough to take my breath away.

I had accomplished all this and never had a boyfriend—I am almost embarrassed to admit this, I never even kissed a boy! I was academically and artistically brilliant, but dumb when it came to male/female relationships. I did have tremendous erotic and sensual energy bubbling under the surface but kept a tight lid on it because of my Christian upbringing. I wanted to stay a virgin until I was married, as the good book said.

I also located a lot of my identity in being the "good girl" in my family. It gave me a sense of pride, to be the one my mother bragged about to her friends. By the time I met my ex-husband at 21, I had only kissed one boy, and I was still traumatized from my first heartbreak—at the hands of a closeted gay boy my freshman year at NYU. For me, my husband was a "good" guy, who was safe for me to be with. I didn't maintain my virginity until the wedding night, but at the time we married, he was the only man I was ever intimate with.

So, six years and one child later, I found myself single again and really dating for the first time. While I spent the first 20 years of my life mastering my mind, I have spent the past 10-plus years connecting to my spirit and learning about myself as a woman. My marriage and the time I've spent dating have been some of my greatest teachers.

I have been to the heavens of ecstasy and to the belly of misery. This book is the outpouring of that journey. Honestly, this is not the book I intended to write. I wanted to write something that espoused a bunch of spiritual ideologies, but I was called to write this. I believe the number one problem many women have is a lack of self-love and trying to find that love through relationships.

When I sat down and talked with my girlfriends, our conversations shifted time and again to issues with men. I realized that most women are needlessly suffering from holding onto men who are no good for them or failing to realize their power to transform their relationships and their lives.

I decided to write this book because I feel like I have mastered this topic over the years, while always open to learning more. After stumbling in the dark and busting my ass many, many times, I have discovered the five steps that can help heal any heartbreak and, most important, open you to the possibilities of new love.

So, whether you just broke up with your boyfriend last week, got stood up last night by the cute guy you met at the club, got played by a guy who used you only for booty calls while you were secretly falling in love, or going through a heartbreaking divorce, this book is for you. Perhaps you are even in a new relationship, but still carrying hurt from a past love. This book is for you too.

I've even had a client who was contemplating ending her relationship, but she read my book, worked on herself, and decided to stay. So no matter where you are on the relationship spectrum, you will get tremendous value from this book.

How to Use This Book

Each chapter in this book is dedicated to a step in the process of getting happy and healed. Within each chapter, there are exercises that support that step. During my healing journey, I studied and benefited from many ancient traditions, including practices from India, China, and Africa. I especially connected to the study of sacred sexuality, the belief that our sexuality is sacred, and we need to have a healthy connection to it to be a balanced and evolved human being.

Many of the exercises featured reflect those studies, while others are of my own creation based on self-help techniques. My work is also strongly rooted in spiritual methods, so if practices such as "meditation" intimidate you or you are simply unfamiliar with them, I ask that you approach the work with an open mind. I believe there is a universal thread of healing through many traditions. In this global age, it deepens our experiences in the world to explore various ways of connecting to the Divine.

This book is meant to aid in your healing, but you are an active participant. I invite you to approach each exercise with honesty and an open heart. Some of what you discover will reaffirm what you already know, and at other times it might surprise you and unveil something you hadn't yet realized. Take your time and be gentle with yourself.

Go through each practice thoughtfully and repeat when necessary. Because I am a big believer in ritual as an organized process of healing, many of the exercises are hands-on and might require you to purchase or have certain items handy. At the beginning of each chapter, I have a list of items you will need to proceed. Review the list and gather what you need, so you can move smoothly through the chapter.

At times the work might get heavy for you as emotions surface. Intimate relationships are our biggest triggers of past pain and trauma. You might need to take a break and come back later. Do that, but keep going. Read and work through each chapter to get the best results possible.

I recommend having a journal, just for this book, and reflecting often through your journey. Also, for chapter three, you will need a jade or yoni egg. This egg, made of semiprecious stone, is key in the healing sacred sexual practices we will do. If you need an egg, please purchase one from my website: letgoletgoddess.com. Also on my site, you can find several resources to help guide you through this book including my Happy and Healed Love Camp, a coaching program where I personally lead you through this journey.

Here are the steps we are going through to get happy, healed, and open to the love we deserve:

1. Let Go!

2. Look in the Mirror

3. Fall in Love with YOU

4. Keep It Moving!

5. Open to the New

Ready to do this work? Time to saddle up, goddesses! Put on your big-girl panties (or a sexy, lace thong) and let's ride!

Items Needed for
Chapter 1
Let Go!

- ✓ Clean piece of white or light-colored cloth

- ✓ White candle

- ✓ Symbols of spiritual significance (cross, ankh, Buddha, angels, etc.)

- ✓ Clear glass container (bowl, cup, vase, etc.)

- ✓ Rocks or sacred gemstones

- ✓ Clean, white shirt and skirt or white dress (inexpensive)

- ✓ Spiritual text you use, if any (Bible, Koran, Bhagavad Gita, affirmation book, etc.)

- ✓ Sage or other purifying incense

- ✓ Sea salt

- ✓ Blue candle

- ✓ Jasmine essential oil

- ✓ Blue flowers

- ✓ Ceramic bowl or iron pot

- ✓ Journal

Chapter 1
Let Go!

"Sometimes letting things go is an act of far greater power than defending or hanging on."

—Eckhart Tolle

I named my company Let Go Let Goddess for a reason. Yes, it has a nice ring to it and rolls sweetly off the tongue. It also has some nice alliteration that the poet in me appreciates, but it is also a commandment, two commandments actually. This chapter just focuses on commandment one: LET GO!

Let go, let go, let go! These two tiny words mean so much. Let go of the man, let go of the relationship. Stop thinking or wishing that it could have played out any differently, surrender to what was. Realize that it unfolded *exactly* as it needed to be to teach you what you needed to know. In the words of author and spiritual teacher Eckhart Tolle,

"Whatever the present moment contains, accept it as if you had chosen it."

I know what you're thinking: "I didn't choose this! Why would I have chosen to be cheated on? To be lied to! To get my heart broken!"

We're going to come to the "why" in chapter two. But, right now, just focus on accepting that it happened. It's over.

You know deep in your heart that you need to let go. This doesn't mean you need to hate him. In fact, you might very well still love him, and love might be why you are still holding on. In fact, you might always love him, which is fine. Some folks believe that when you really love someone, you never stop. However, you still need to release the relationship.

Before you commit to step one, letting go, you must really know in your heart that the relationship is over, and it's time to move on. This is not something I can tell you; only you can make that decision. If you're not sure that you're ready to let go of this relationship, then I invite you to do some soul work.

Is It Really Over?

When I was making the decision to leave my marriage, I experienced a lot of turmoil. My emotions flipped me back and forth like a tempest. I went to everybody to get advice about what I should do. I was so torn. What made it even more difficult was that I knew I was hurting my husband. He did not want our relationship to end.

Getting hurt by someone is terrible, but hurting someone you care about makes you feel equally horrible. I felt guilty. How many women even get a chance to be married?

The voice inside of me said, "Marriage is rare in this day and age! Lawd knows marriage for a *Black* woman is like winning the golden ticket to Willy Wonka's Chocolate Factory! Chile', are you crazy?!"

I also had a son, how could I take him away from his father?

I went on a search outside myself, trying to find out what to do. I went to my spiritual teachers, but no one would make a decision for me. They only told me that they would support me in whatever I decided to do. Finally, my spiritual mother told me to go light a candle, ask God, and meditate on what decision I should make.

I did, and, shortly after, I had a dream. I dreamed I was getting on an elevator at a construction site. There was a bunch of other people also on the elevator. At the last minute, something told me to get off the elevator, and I did. The elevator began going up, and as it did, it got stuck. The folks in it were dangling dangerously overhead. I woke up, and my decision about my marriage was made.

I knew the elevator was a symbol of my marriage. The people in it represented what society or what everyone else was doing, and it needed to be "reconstructed." Due to fear, most folks go along in situations they know they should leave and wind up getting stuck. I knew in my heart, I wouldn't become the woman I desired to be if I stayed in my marriage. In fact, I had only scratched the surface of who that woman was. I felt my partner and I were on two different paths, and we would be happier going our separate ways, while remaining united in the raising of our son.

So if you're hovering in limbo, I invite you to do this soul work meditation. It may well be that you need to work through your differences with your significant other and hold onto your relationship. It could be that you jump from man to man, only to encounter the same issues, because you're constantly running when the going gets tough.

The purpose of our being in relationships is to grow. We come together to evolve one another's souls. We meet one another along our journeys as assignments, so whether he was a one-night stand or a long-term boyfriend, he came to teach you a lesson. Is your assignment with each other over? There is no magic checklist I can give you to tell you that, no hard and fast rules, only your heart can give you the truth.

Even if you already think you KNOW the relationship is over, I still encourage you to do this meditation to go deeper. We are going to start by setting up our sacred space or altar.

Creating a Sacred Space

Altars or sacred spaces have existed for thousands of years, and practically every spiritual system has some sort of version of this. We create altars to have a sanctified area to commune with the Divine. When we engage in doing our spiritual work in the same area, that space becomes energized, and it allows us to connect to Spirit much more easily.

In this book, I will assign different meditations and rituals to be done at your altar. The idea of having altars and doing rituals might be strange to some of us in Western cultures, but these kinds of spiritual practices were intrinsic in all ancient societies. Unfortunately, Hollywood and Western cultures have demonized many indigenous practices and wrongfully associated them with "devil worship," which is highly false and grossly ignorant.

As a student, initiate, and practitioner of a variety of indigenous spiritual sciences, the use of altars and ritual is central to the healing work I prescribe. However, I am not asking you to switch or change to whom or what you pray to. These practices are general prescriptions gleaned from my studies and not part of one specific religion.

Interestingly enough, nowadays many Westerners are looking to the ancient practices of our ancestors to heal their ruptured selves. Many are slowly waking up to the failure of the intellect or technology to solve all our problems. People are rediscovering the power of rituals. Sobonfu E. Some, a teacher of ancient wisdom from the Dagara tribe of West Africa, writes in her book, *Welcoming Spirit Home: Ancient African Teachings to Celebrate Children and Community,*

"Ritual helps us to remove blocks between us and our true spirit. The purpose of rituals is to take us to a place of self-discovery and mastery. In this sense ritual is to the soul what food is to the physical body" (p. 24).

With those intentions of feeding our souls, let's begin!

I am going to give you basic directions for setting up an altar; feel free to add or take away from it as you wish.

First, select a table or surface to create it on. The table can be as small or large as you like, depending on how elaborate you want it to be. Being a New Yorker, I deal with limited space, so, my favorite places for altars are the tops of dressers, since they're already a part of my furniture. Or you can use a mantel piece or a bookcase.

Next select a nice, clean piece of white or light-colored cloth. Allow your spirit to guide you in the color. White is a great color, because it radiates a peaceful energy. Blue is often used for healing, as well as green. Yellow can inspire creativity or joy.

Once you have selected your cloth, please gather some candles. For a lot of our work, I'll prescribe a basic white candle enclosed in a glass case. They are often called seven-day candles and can be found in most drugstores or botanicas (a store that specializes in herbs or spiritual items). You might also want to have other colors available, such as blue, pink, yellow, red, or green. We will use a variety of different colors throughout our work. Color therapy is a well-known methodology in psychology and spiritual science.

You might wish to have a spiritual symbol on your altar, such as a cross, ankh, Buddha, goddess statue, angel, etc.

Images and pictures of serene places in nature, such as an ocean or a waterfall could be used to invoke relaxation. It is also good to keep fresh water in a clear glass (no plastic) bowl, cup, or vase on the altar. The water acts as a spiritual conduit and brings a cooling energy.

Rocks or stones on an altar can bring a grounding energy. Take a walk through the park and look for some rocks that "speak" to you. Some people place four rocks around their altar to represent the four directions. Crystals are also great conduits of energy and can be placed on your altar. You might also want to have beautiful flowers there to bring in positive energy and a sweet fragrance.

If you have a spiritual book you like to use, such as the Bible, Koran, Bhagavad Gita, affirmation book, etc., you can also place that on your altar. When you sit and say your prayers or meditate, you can receive messages by reading a passage from these books. A practice that I like is to ask for clarity about an issue I'm having. Then I open one of my books at random, and read the passage from the page. I always get some wonderful messages that speak exactly to what I'm going through.

Once you have gathered your altar items, you want to purify your space. Wipe the surface with warm, soapy water and use incense, such as sage, to energetically clean it. Then with intention, place each item on your altar, starting with the cloth. You might want to say a prayer and bless each item as you put it down.

For example, when placing the water you might say, "May Spirit bless this water, so that it might bring coolness and peace."

For the rocks, you could ask, "God, will you bless these rocks, that they will bring stability and groundedness to my life?"

Understand that all these items are symbolic and represent the elements of nature: water, fire, earth, air, etc. These elements are within us, so when we tap into the power of nature, we are tapping into the same forces that are also in us to bring balance and harmony to our lives.

Now that your sacred space is created, you should feel a sense of peace and relaxation whenever you go near it. Remember, you can add or take away from any of the items I mentioned. The items you use on your altar are as individual and as varied as you are as a human being. Think of your altar as a beautiful elevated reflection of you and the energy you want to create in your life on a daily basis.

Now we're ready to move on to our first Soul Work Assignment.

Soul Work Assignment #1
Relationship Transition and Purpose

Tools: White clothes, white candle, journal

Preparation: Find a quiet evening to do this exercise—put the kids to sleep and the phone on vibrate. Play some relaxing music, maybe flute or ocean sounds. Take a nice hot shower or bath. Find some comfortable white clothes to wear. White is important because it is a neutral color that purifies your energy field. When you meditate you want to feel as clear and peaceful as possible, and the color white naturally encourages this.

Meditation: Once you bathe and dress, light a white candle on your altar. Sit in front of your altar with the lit candle. It is important that you are sitting up straight in a chair that supports your back, with your feet flat on the floor. You can also sit up on the edge of your bed, if your altar is in your bedroom. Unless you are a dope yogi who can maintain lotus position, it is easier to relax when sitting up straight with a back support—add pillows, if needed. The most important thing is that you are comfortable. However, do not lie down on the bed, as you do not want to fall asleep.

Set your intention for the meditation. This can be done through prayer or quietly speaking to Spirit in your mind.

Ask God/Goddess/the ancestors, or to whom you pray, to show you if it is time to leave this relationship or if you should stay. Ask that it be revealed to you if this person is the right one for you to be with at this time. Also ask that the lesson and purpose behind this relationship be revealed to you, so that you might fulfill whatever spiritual assignment you were given.

Close your eyes, and bring your attention to your belly. You should be breathing slowly and deeply from your abdomen. On the in breath, your belly goes out, on the out breath, your belly comes in. Your breath should not be locked in the upper chest region, that's where we breathe from when we're upset. You want your breath to be slow, deep, and rhythmic.

Continue breathing and floating with the music. Watch the thoughts that come without judging them or trying to stop them. A voice might be telling you this is stupid, or that you're too tired to do this; be as indifferent to the thoughts as you would to cars passing on a highway—just watch them.

As you continue to breathe and relax, you should feel a sense of peace. Gradually, the thoughts might start receding into white noise, and underneath that noise you might perceive other things happening. Try to tune into any images or messages that give you a clue about the relationship. You might feel a need to cry or release any emotions coming up. Allow yourself to do so. Do not try and force any result.

The most important thing is that you have asked the universe to give you an answer, and you're implanting that desire deep within your spirit. You cannot predict how that answer will unfold. You might get a message through meditation, or have a dream, like I did. The person might suddenly just disappear from your life; a friend or maybe even a perfect stranger will speak a truth to you so clearly that you will know it is the Divine speaking through them to you. You also might just have a crystal-clear resolve that your relationship is over, no longer feeling torn and confused.

Sit in meditation for about 20 minutes, or however long feels comfortable. Write in your journal anything that came up for you; include any feelings, messages, or emotions. Try to go right to bed after you complete this Soul Work Assignment. I do not encourage you to talk on the phone or watch TV. You want to take this deep into the subconscious, and the best way to do that is to go to sleep. Trust that your answer is coming, if it hasn't already.

Once You Know It's Over

Ok, now that you've done the work, you should be clear whether or not this relationship has transitioned, and you should also have a clue about the lesson behind the relationship. We will go more into this in chapter two, but you should have some understanding of what this relationship was teaching you, or you've wasted your time.

Life is just like school, when we fail to learn our lessons we have to repeat the grade! We want to keep progressing as much as possible, so make sure you have the lesson. Now, I know some women might be holding on to a shred of hope that there's still a possibility that you might get back together. Aren't there couples who break up for a while, then come back together and get married?

This is true, there are times when a couple might need a break to sort things out and grow, and then decide to come together again. If this is what you're thinking, only time will tell. I encourage you to do the work in this book anyway, despite any hope of reconciliation. As the saying goes, "You cannot lose what truly belongs to you." So, yes, if the relationship is meant to be, it will be.

However, you are obviously out of alignment with each other right now, or you wouldn't be broken up in the first place. If you get back together, without working on yourself,

I guarantee you it will be disastrous. Do the work, and let life unfold. Whatever will be, will be.

~~~~~

So, now, we are going to focus on letting go. This doesn't mean that you can't ever see this person again or you two can't be friends, but, for the time being, you're going to need to create some space between yourself and this person.

Obviously, if you have children with him, you're going to need to communicate about them. It is important, in cases that involve children, that you come to an agreement on how you're going to handle the issue of your child. Please do not ever use your child to get back at him. I hate hearing of cases of hurt mothers using the child to punish the father. Please refrain from any petty behaviors, as we work on healing the deeper wounds. Only communicate about the child and do not get into any back-and-forth discussion about the relationship, once you've decided it's over.

~~~~~

Now, no matter how long or short the relationship was, if you're reading this book it means that your energy has somehow bonded with this person's energy. The reason why breakups are so hard and can leave us feeling so empty inside is because our energy has intertwined with another's energy. We become dependent on their energy to feel whole. This is why couples yo-yo through cycles of making up and breaking up.

We literally become addicted to the other person, and like with any drug, when it's taken away, we go through a withdrawal period. So, you might feel absolutely depressed for days, or even weeks, as your energy recalibrates itself and becomes balanced again. It's like when you're using GPS navigation and you make a wrong turn; the device takes a minute to recalculate and get you back on the right track again.

But don't worry, I'm here to guide you every step of the way. As you find a new direction, the road might be bumpy at first, but trust me, where we're going is a beautiful place filled with peace and possibility.

Many people often neglect the true power of sexual energy. If you've been intimate with the person, then your energies have blended in the deepest form possible. Especially if you got to the point where you and your mate no longer used safe sex protection and were exchanging energies "raw." A really intense connection is forged when our sacred fluids are exchanged. So please understand that it's normal to feel "down" or like you just need one more "hit," but realize that this relationship has transitioned and no longer serves you.

I understand; it is not often easy to make a clean break and "sex with the ex" can be a comfortable thing to fall into, but it is not always wise. If you do make a mistake, don't beat yourself up about it. One of my favorite spiritual teachers, Abraham Hicks, always says,

"You can never get it done and you can never get it wrong."

What this means is that we're always learning. If you rebound, there's another lesson you are working on. I firmly believe that when we're truly ready to move on, we will. Other times, life will give us a swift kick in the butt to let us know we need to recalibrate.

Listen, because as the saying goes,

"A hard head makes a soft behind."

Social Media and Drunken Texts

We now have covert ways to "stalk" our exes in this day and age of social media—or sometimes, we're the one being watched. Reading his status updates, where he is flirting with other women, staring at his pictures online, seeing who he's following on Instagram, or combing over his tweets is not going to help you to let go! I say it all the time that Facebook is the "devil," because it has the ability to cause all kinds of confusion and emotional turmoil, just because someone liked so-and-so's picture.

Now, I'm not saying you need to unfriend your ex. You don't have to obliterate this person from your life, but if you know it's going to trigger you during your healing stage, you sure as hell can hide them from your newsfeed! You're in triage now, baby girl, so feel free to remove anything that could cause a relapse. You can always unhide him later, when it's no longer a sore point for you. (If you follow all my steps, it will certainly not be!) Of course, if it's too painful, or you're being harassed, feel free to unfriend or block him.

I also advise against drunken or crazy texting, please save yourself from the following morning of regret. You don't need to tell him what's on your mind, curse him out one last time, or anything else for that matter. If you feel a need to give him a piece of your mind through the phone, write it in your notepad and save it for our Soul Work Assignment #2. If he's texting you things that make you feel uncomfortable, or that are inappropriate now that you've broken up, kindly ask him to stop. If he refuses, block his number.

It's important that you maintain your boundaries. If he has moved on and now has another girlfriend or girlfriends— stay out of their lives! You don't need to "warn" her about him. If he was cheating on somebody else with you, it's not your job to give her all the details of your relationship and how he's a lying dog. Let the universe do its job, everything that needs to be revealed is always revealed in time. Above all, carry yourself with dignity and respect like the goddess you are!

Relationship Memorabilia

What should you do with all the tokens and memorabilia from the relationship? Your mate and you might have exchanged books, gifts, cards, jewelry, etc. I do not necessarily recommend you get a trash bag and throw it all away, unless that is what your spirit is telling you to do to really clear the space. But, if every time you look at them it makes you sad or angry, I do suggest packing those things away and getting them out of sight for the time being.

I still have pictures from when my ex-husband and I were dating. I didn't throw them away, because I felt like that experience was an important part of my journey. However, they are in a drawer stored away, and I don't take them out and lament over the relationship—that is unhealthy. So you have to decide whether you want to completely bury this person and get rid of any symbols or trinkets, or pack them away as memories of an experience that you learned from. This is totally up to you!

Clearing Out the Past

So, now that we know the relationship is over, and we have an idea of the lesson it taught, and we have cleaned out or put away reminders of the past relationship, it is now time to energetically clear away our bond to our former partner.

Soul Work Assignment #2
Relationship Clearing Ritual

Tools: Incense (I recommend dried sage. It is usually sold tied in little bundles. Sage is an herb that's great for healing and cleansing. It was frequently used in Native American cleansing ceremonies. Frankincense and myrrh are good also. These have ancient and biblical symbolism and have been used for thousands of years to cleanse negative energy and bring blessings. I love to use the frankincense incense that comes in little rocks that are burned directly on charcoal.)

- ✓ Two cups sea salt or one liter ocean water
- ✓ Blue flowers
- ✓ Seven drops jasmine essential oil
- ✓ Matches or a lighter
- ✓ Paper and pen
- ✓ A ceramic or iron pot
- ✓ White clothes
- ✓ White and/or blue candle
- ✓ A clean house
- ✓ Small/medium rocks (optional)

Preparation: Before doing the ritual to release your energetic bond to your partner, you will need to do a cleansing bath. Cleansing or spiritual baths are a well-known healing practice, particularly within traditions of the African Diaspora. I will be sharing different kinds of baths throughout this book. This is a simple bath, but you can make it as complex as you want and add whatever different things your spirit tells you (that is, certain gemstones or herbs you're familiar with).

Healing Bath

First, take a quick shower to remove the physical dirt from your body. The bath will be to remove the energetic sludge.

Light your candles and run your bath water. As the water is running, add the sea salt. Sea salt purifies your spirit and body, helping to relieve stress and relax tired muscles. While adding the salt, pray your intentions into the water. Ask Spirit to cleanse you of all negative energy that is clinging to you and take away that which you no longer need (your past relationship) and bring to you something better.

Once the bath is full, add seven drops of jasmine oil. Jasmine works to raise self-esteem, and it heals the heart chakra. It is also good for nasal and lung conditions and will stimulate mental clarity and practicality. It has a soft, feminine, nurturing effect. As you sprinkle the oil into the water, ask for healing of your heart from all present and past pain, hurt, and resentment. You can even rub a drop over your heart.

Sprinkle petals from the blue flowers directly into the water. The color blue is associated with healing, nurturing, and the Mother Goddess. Ask her to nurture you with her love.

Depending on the time of the year or where you live, you can also collect some water from the ocean and add it to your bath. The water from the sea has natural healing properties within it. (As a side note, if you CAN take a trip to the ocean prior to this cleansing ritual, I highly recommend it. Spend a quiet day by yourself or maybe go with a girlfriend and get into the cleansing energy of the ocean. In many ancient traditions, the ocean is connected to the Divine Mother spirit of the world. You can say a prayer while at the ocean and ask the Great Mother of All to help you heal. If you take water from the ocean, leave a simple offering of seven pennies or even flowers or fruit thanking her for the healing energy.)

Soak in the bath for at least 30 minutes. While soaking, you can listen to your healing music or ocean sounds. Continue to pray and meditate, asking Spirit to lift that which you no longer need. You can take the blue flower petals and rub them against your body, while you pray for healing.

It is good during this bath if tears come, because this is a release. Allow your tears to cleanse you, as they are salty, just like the healing waters of the ocean. You are working on letting go of wounds, not only from the past relationship, but all relationships you might be energetically still hanging on to.

After soaking in the bath, let the water drain and imagine all the residue of the past leaving with the water. Once finished, get dressed in your whites and gather your ritual items.

Ritual

Your house should be clean. You are going to burn the incense and walk with it around the house, saying prayers and asking all the negative energy to leave. Open the windows to allow in fresh air. Focus on the entrances, exits, and corners of your house. If there is a particular part of the house, where you and your ex had an argument or any other stressful event, pay special attention to that area. Also make sure to smudge the bedroom and the bed if you slept together there.

Be sure to wave the incense over your body to purify your aura—do the bottoms of your feet and other spiritual entrances and exits (hands, knees, between your legs, under your arms, etc.) Stay mindful of the sage, which can get really

smoky. When you feel that the space is significantly
you can put the incense out.

Dressed in your whites, sit in front of your altar or s
space with your candles lit. Take the paper and pen. You are
going to write a letter to your ex. (If you're carrying wounds
from more than one man, you can write more than one letter.
Feel free to write a letter to ALL your exes, if you know you
are still carrying wounds.)

In your letter, you are going to say WHATEVER it is that
you need to get off your chest. Pretend as if you are talking to
him and let go of the words you need to release. This is not
about censoring yourself or trying to sound "spiritual." This
is about getting it out! Tell him how you are feeling, why the
relationship is over, and that you wish for the energetic bond
between you two to be released. Once you say all that you
need to, thank him for the opportunity and the lesson he
came to teach you. Wish him light and love, as you both
move on with the rest of your lives.

Next, get your ceramic bowl or iron pot. If you want to
protect the bottom of it, you can line it with rocks. You are
going to say a prayer, asking Spirit to be present as you
energetically release this man from your life. Fold the letter
and place it in the pot. Take a match and light fire to the
letter.

As you watch it burn, imagine that your intention is being
transmuted in the fire and the past relationship is being
released. Trust that even though you might not be "speaking"
these words to your ex, that the energy is being felt, and the
connection you had is being transformed in the fire.

Once the letter has completely burned, you should feel a
big relief. Feel free to meditate after this, or go directly to
sleep. You should sleep well. Pay attention to any dreams you
might have or experiences you have during the next several
days.

Forgiveness

There is a quote that says,

"Not forgiving someone is like drinking poison and expecting the other person to die."

Holding onto anger toward your ex is going to hurt you more than it hurts him. Most of the time, the person we are mad at doesn't have any idea of the intensity of our feelings, nor are they affected by it. We are harmed much more than they are. So forgiveness is really an act of self-emancipation; you want to get to the point where seeing the person or hearing their name is no longer a trigger for you.

Yes, this does take time. In fact, I do believe anger at the beginning of a breakup can be healthy. There is intelligence behind our emotions, and usually, when we feel angry, it is because we have allowed a boundary to be crossed.

So, if you are angry, what boundary did you allow the relationship to cross?

Were you always the one *doing* for the other person, working to please them while ignoring yourself?

Did you always pay for everything?

Did you forsake yourself because you were so wrapped up in your partner?

A lot of women behave like this, because they feel this will bring them love. We often want someone to be around us so desperately, that we will lower our standards, stop doing things we love, and even carry men financially just to have someone in our beds at night. Then we get angry when this person takes full advantage of us, when we were the one allowing the behavior, and sometimes even encouraging it. In chapter two, we will get into the "why" behind such actions, but for now let's just focus on letting go and forgiveness.

Forgiveness does not mean the other person is absolved from what they did; it means that you are emotionally free and no longer controlled by the past. We have to trust life and know that everyone "reaps what they sow." The saying "what comes around, goes around" is a universal law.

Forgiving someone does not mean they are no longer accountable for their actions, but it's not up to YOU to even the score. Let the Divine do its job. Quite frankly, life is our greatest teacher and has the power to balance things much better than we can. Also, know that nobody is being "punished," as we ALL receive the energy we put into the universe!

I remember when I first moved out of the apartment I shared with my ex-husband. I had tremendous guilt for leaving the marriage. I felt bad because he was angry with me for not staying and blamed me for ripping our family apart. Though I knew I was doing the right thing, it still felt so awful.

I remember one night, while meditating on letting go of the hurt feelings I harbored toward my husband, I heard my higher self tell me that while forgiving him was important, I needed to also forgive myself. We carry guilt when we are afraid of living our authentic truth; we present a false version of our self to not cause conflict with others.

This, of course, does not work, so when the truth of who we really are surfaces, people feel they have been misled. Many of us carry, for a long time, the shame of not being true to ourselves. Though in leaving my marriage, I was not in fact "wrong," I needed to release the guilt and forgive myself for feeling that I was causing him pain by doing what was best for me. I knew my husband needed a different kind of woman; he would be much happier with someone else as I could not give him what he was looking for. I also knew I needed to be with a different kind of man, and, even more, discover what kind of man I really wanted.

My higher self also told me that there was nothing to be forgiven! There was a part of me that no one could touch, a part of me that was whole and complete. The same thing applied to my husband. I needed to forgive myself for thinking I could even hurt him; he also has a part of him that is infallible and cannot be harmed. So, if we can't be hurt, what within us feels the pain of a perceived betrayal? It is the ego.

The ego is the part of us that identifies with things such as money, status, education, relationships, etc. The ego bases its identity on things outside itself; so when something is removed, the ego feels pain. In a relationship, our ego is happy because often we are basing our self-worth on the relationship. Once out of a relationship, the ego is mad because it feels a loss—the identity has nothing to stand on. We suffer anger and depression because the ego has been starved of its status symbol.

So what must we do? We must base our identity on our higher self! Our higher self is that divine part within us from which nothing can be added to, and nothing can be taken away. We are born complete and whole! No relationship or lack thereof can change that. So yes, forgive yourself and forgive others, because, in fact, you are unmovable and unshakeable!

Keep in mind that I'm not saying this to discount your feelings or experiences. I'm not one of those people who think that the ego is "evil" and needs to be overcome. Sometimes it hurts, and that's real! I am saying this as a reminder for *you* to get in alignment with You!

There is a reservoir of peace and power within you that no one can subtract from. We don't have to go through life holding onto anger or hurt based on what someone did to us. We also do not need to walk around haunted by guilt. If you're having issues with forgiveness of self or others, try these affirmations. Affirmations are statements of power that help to plant proper ideas or beliefs into our minds.

Forgiveness Affirmations

1. I release all pain of the past and step peacefully into the power of my now.

2. I forgive all others and myself, knowing that in truth nothing can be added to me, and nothing can be taken away from me. I am complete.

3. I am connected to a great love that heals any and all hurt. I allow this love to fill my soul, knowing that it is my true nature. I am free from all past painful experiences and radiate infinite light to all beings.

These affirmations can be used during meditations and throughout the day when you catch yourself having an angry thought or flashback. You can also write your own affirmations about forgiveness.

As you begin to change your thinking and see forgiveness not as a weakness, but as a tool for greater expansion, strength, and love, you will notice dynamic shifts in your life. Once your past no longer has a hold on you, you are more fully present to accept the gifts of the now and open to the road of the future.

Now that we have learned to let go and forgive, we can move on to delving even *deeper*. Yes, it's going to get even deeper! The next chapter is perhaps one of the most important chapters in this entire book. Let's take out our magic mirrors and have a look to see what's really going on inside our hearts.

Items Needed for
Chapter 2
Look in the Mirror

- ✓ Journal
- ✓ White and/or blue candle
- ✓ Incense
- ✓ White clothing
- ✓ Rocks

Chapter 2
Look in the Mirror

"Your mate is your mirror."

—Unknown

I was curled up in my bed, clutching a pillow with darkness as my only companion. My tears had carved a river down my cheeks and my eyes were puffy. It was three days until New Year's Eve, and I was not going to be spending it with the man I loved. He was going to be spending it with *her*. I found out through a Facebook status that he was having a New Year's Eve party. Later that night, when I went over to visit and curiously asked him about it, he told me in a matter of fact way that it was *her* birthday, and I couldn't come. I was crushed.

Of course, technically he wasn't "my man," we had an "understanding." He wasn't "ready" for a relationship; he told me he didn't want anyone to "own" him. We both agreed that we could see other people, but secretly I wanted him to be the only one. Every time he texted me, my heart fluttered with excitement. When I asked him what he was doing, I prayed that he would invite me over. When he did, I was in heaven, but when he told me he was busy, I lamented in my own private hell, scared that he was with another woman.

Meanwhile, this man NEVER took me out on a date or publicly demonstrated any sort of real affection for me. Our relationship consisted of me going over to his house late at night, or him coming over to mine, and us having sex. Oh, we did have great conversations. He was actually really talented and brilliant. I made excuses for the nature of our relationship. I told myself "He's a struggling artist; he can't afford to take me out, all that really matters is that we spend quality time together."

But when I found out that he was throwing a bash for his other lady friend, I felt like a total fool. You know what they say about New Year's Eve, if you're not with your "man" on New Year's Eve, then he's not your man! I realized that all his talk about lack of funds and being really "private" about his relationships was just that: talk.

He wasn't completely unavailable. He was just unavailable to me—a hard pill to swallow.

"how far have you walked for men who've never held your feet in their laps?
how often have you bartered with bone, only to sell yourself short?
why do you find the unavailable so alluring?
where did it begin? what went wrong? and who made you feel so worthless?"

—Warsan Shire
"Questions For the Woman I Was Last Night"

This part of a poem, so beautifully articulated by Warsan Shire, conveys a truth many women need to hear. Many of us are in a trance with the "unavailable" man, the one who cannot give us the love, honor, and respect we truly want. We are an open buffet for these men, offering all of our selves, while often receiving and demanding little in return. On the other hand, the man who would do anything for us, we shun and walk away from.

Caught in a cycle of attracting unavailable men, we often repeatedly get our hearts broken. These men want to enjoy the benefits of being in a relationship with you—the sex and companionship—but at the same time refuse to really commit to you. When it's convenient for them, or when they feel like you're getting too "clingy," they will remind you that you are not their "girl," or they just vanish for a few days, weeks, or even months until you cool off.

When they return, you're so happy they've come back (because it must mean that they really care) that you again get caught up in the entire cycle, hoping they'll decide to make you "the one." If you snag one of these men, even though he gives you the title of "girlfriend," you might experience that he is still emotionally uncommitted to you. You might have the physical man, but the relationship leaves you unfulfilled, because he isn't truly opening his heart to you.

Shire asks some important questions,

where did it begin?

what went wrong?

who made you feel so worthless?

This chapter, "Look in the Mirror," is going to help you answer these questions. You're going to take out your magical mirror and discover how you attracted this person into your life in the first place. Many women often tend to date or be in relationships with the same type of man, just in a different body. So, what is your pattern when it comes to men? Who do you attract?

Is it one of the following men?

Mr. Unavailable, who has no desire to commit to you either physically or emotionally?

Mr. Cheater, who can't keep his dick in his pants?

Mr. Pathological Liar, who invents stories that Hollywood would envy?

Mr. Broke, who can't hold down a job?

Mr. Control Freak, who needs to know what you're doing, who you're talking to, and where you're at every minute of the day?

I could go on and on. What are your dominant patterns when it comes to men? (It is also a well-noted fact that women in abusive relationships tend to repeatedly attract abusers. If you have a pattern of attracting either verbally or physically abusive men, along with the exercises in this book, I strongly suggest you also seek professional counseling to aid in your healing.)

Soul Work Assignment #3
What's My Pattern?

Tools: Paper and pen, honesty

Preparation: You might want to sit in front of your altar and do some breathing to first center yourself. Try breathing slowly in and out for five minutes to clear your mind.

Process

On a sheet of paper, choose your three most significant past romantic relationships. As I've stated before, it doesn't matter how long these relationships lasted. A one-night stand or even a high school crush can have a lasting effect on your energetic patterns.

All that matters is how much they affected you. Think about your most emotionally charged relationships with men who have had a significant impact on you.

On your paper, divide it into three columns with each guy's name at the top:

Person A | Person B | Person C

Under each column, write a short narrative about each relationship, focusing on the following:

Beginning: How did you meet? What attracted you to this person?

Middle: What was the major problem/conflict that happened? What issues came up in the relationship?

End: How and why did the relationship end?

Write about this for each person. Try to do it in a way that does not get caught up in the story. You don't need to get lost in all the details (we've let go, remember?). Just state the facts. Here's an example:

Larry
(aka Mr. Unavailable Struggling Artist)

Met at a poetry reading. Was attracted to his sense of humor and talent at performing poetry. We exchanged numbers and hooked up shortly after that.

Did not want commitment, yet continued to have intimate relationship and dated for more than a year. A lot of jealousy on both sides and many arguments about why he wouldn't commit.

Relationship ended when I found out he actually had a girlfriend, and I no longer would settle for being a "side chick."

~~~~~

Once you write a narrative for each man, look for patterns. Underline things in your story that these relationships had in common. Did most of these men cheat on you? Were they all unavailable? Try to find common themes and events, even if at first it might not seem similar.

Ask Spirit to guide you. If you're not finding a pattern, perhaps you've picked the wrong men to focus on for this assignment. If there is a man among the three who stands out from the rest, were there men before or after him who were similar? Really go deep in this exploration to find out your pattern. Once you feel like you've narrowed it and can see what the pattern is, or the patterns are, write it in a sentence. For example,

"My relationship pattern has been to attract unavailable men who use me for sex."

"My relationship pattern has been to attract men who cheat on me and lie to me."

"My pattern is to have really intense relationships with men that don't last long."

A Note on This Soul Work Assignment: This exercise will probably stir some strong emotions within you. It's ok if it does. Repeat the forgiveness affirmations you learned in the last chapter. The exercise is not meant to "point the finger" or blame these men. It is definitely not to blame yourself either! It's to identify the patterns showing up in your life, so you can transform and attract the real love you want. However, you have to do the work. Now that you know what your patterns are, let's find out where the root of these patterns lie.

What if I told you that Larry was just my creation? I made him up! No, not in a fictional way, everything I shared with you actually happened. He was my creation, because everything that transpired in our relationship—from him not wanting to "commit," to the other girl, to us not ever going out on a date—was, in fact, a reflection of something deep within me. What if I told you that he was my mirror and reflected patterns and beliefs within myself that I needed to shift?

Yes, it's true! To quote Iyanla Vanzant,

*"The people who come into our lives are
a reflection of who we are.
They reveal those things we cannot or
refuse to see about ourselves."*

Every man that you've ever been with is your reflection in some kind of way. If we don't like what our relationships are reflecting back to us, then to get a different image, we must change ourselves! This is why many of us date the same kind of men, there is an energetic pattern that we are emitting that is calling this man to us. So to get a better reflection, we must first understand where the root of this pattern started.

The law of attraction states that "like attracts like," meaning that whatever energy we project through our thoughts, mental images, and behaviors will eventually be drawn back to us. For example, people who complain about not having any money will often remain broke. Women who believe that "there are no good men" will stay single or caught up in a bad relationship with a "no-good man."

The energy that we put into the universe is what's going to show up on our doorstep every time. Even the Bible states,

"Death and life are in the power of the tongue."

—Proverbs 18:21
New American Standard Bible

Our words, which ultimately reflect our thoughts and beliefs, have power.

In terms of relationships, we often are operating from subconscious desires and beliefs that attract certain kinds of people to us. Quite often, these beliefs were implanted within us when we were too young to realize what we were taking in. We then spend much of our adult life unknowingly acting out these inherited patterns.

In this soul work process, we are going to delve deeply into our past relationships to figure out how we attracted these men and how they are our reflection.

Soul Work Assignment #4
Mirror, Mirror

Tools: Pen and paper, readiness for dynamic change

Preparation: Make sure you have a significant amount of time for this. This could and should get extremely deep for you. Take a shower to clear your aura of things you might have picked up throughout the day or week. Wear comfortable clothes, and do some breathing before you start.

I also suggest you have a close girlfriend or someone you trust to talk to once you finish this process. This could happen the same day or the next day. It is important for you to have some support, for what you discover should cause a dynamic shift in your life. As women, being able to talk through our feelings is important. Make sure you have someone you can do this with.

I am available for private coaching, if you feel more comfortable relating to me. You may contact me through my web page, letgoletgoddess.com.

Process

Go back and look at the men from your "What's My Pattern?" assignment. For now, choose one man to work with. If you desire, you can go back and complete this "Mirror, Mirror" assignment for each man, but for right now, choose the one most significant to you. This could be the man you just recently ended a relationship with or another one who had a greater impact. Whoever it is, should be directly related to the pattern you identified as your relationship pattern. If you have more than one pattern, for now, choose just one to work with. Often these patterns are connected to one another anyway.

Write the person's name at the top of the paper. Divide the paper into two columns.

In column one, write "What I Liked/Loved."

In column two, write "What I Did Not Like/What Hurt Me."

Man's Name

What I Liked/Loved—What I Did Not Like/What Hurt Me

In the column of "What I Liked/Loved" make a list of everything you really enjoyed about this person. Don't front, it wasn't all bad! This person had to have some characteristics that attracted you in the first place. Go beyond looks (unless your pattern is tied up in physical image). What were the traits that really drew you to this person? Write them down.

Then, after you have listed everything, think about the best times of the relationship, how did you feel? Most likely you felt beautiful, sexy, and on top of the world. Write how you felt. For example,

Larry

What I Liked/Loved

- His sense of humor

- His great artistic talent

- He was fun

- He was very motivated to complete his life goals

- Made me feel happy and alive

So here is the reflection, the positive characteristics that this person possessed represent the underdeveloped traits you have. The things you loved about this person are the hidden gems you were subconsciously hoping to bring out in yourself by connecting to him. These qualities represent your yet-to-be-realized potential.

The way you felt when things were "good" around your ex reflects how you truly wish to feel once these gifts are developed in your life. This is why being around certain men or people can be addictive or intoxicating. We subconsciously recognize something in another that we want in ourselves, so we "fall in love" with this unrealized potential we see reflected to us. Often we neglect to develop these traits within ourselves, because we are too focused on the other person to make us "feel good." Ideally, what happens is that this latent part of us gets strengthened because of the relationship with this person.

In the example of Larry, he had a brilliant mind and was a great poet, well-known in the spoken-word community. I connected with him at a time when I was rediscovering my artistic talent, and he helped me a great deal with my poetry. He was also a lot of fun. Having just left my marriage, where I had been rigid and unhappy, he was a welcome release. With him, I learned how to let go, be spontaneous, and have fun.

Once you realize what the positive reflection about the man was, write it in a sentence or two. For example,

"My relationship with Larry reflects my desire to be artistically brilliant and developed. I want to feel celebrated and recognized. I want to live a free life full of fun."

~~~~~

We can leave this situation like it is for now, however, we'll come back to how to cultivate our self in chapter four, "Keep It Moving!" But I want you to realize that you have the power to make yourself feel the way he made you feel. This person came as a beautiful reflection of your potential, and, now that you know what it is, you are free to develop this within yourself, if this characteristic trait is something that you still are working on, of course.

We change and grow, so sometimes what we once wanted no longer fits, and this can also mark why certain people disappear from our lives. I just want you to understand how this person was a positive reflection of something deep within you, and no matter how great they made you feel, you can tap into that by developing yourself.

Ok, now that we know what turned us *on* about our ex, let's look at what turned us *off* and hurt us. Make a list of all the behaviors and traits that you did not like about your partner. Especially think of the things that caused you the most pain because, often, these are our deepest reflections. For example,

Larry

What I Did Not Like/ What Hurt Me

- Would often not answer calls and texts

- Emotionally unavailable; did not verbally express his feelings for me or show them

- Lied about where he was and who he was seeing

- Refused to commit to me, not ready for a relationship

Life is wonderful, in that it always provides us with opportunities to grow through challenges. Often our intimate partners cause us the most pain, because they are the people who bring out our "stuff" most easily.

What we are often unaware of is that we have attracted this person to us for this very reason—to show us what lies within us that is ready to be released, healed, and elevated.

So look at your list of what you didn't like and try to find the reflection. Often when someone does something that really riles us up, it is because of one of these things:

1. **They are showing us what we expect.**

2. **They are mirroring back our behavior to us.**

3. **They are treating us the way we treat ourselves.**

4. **Their behavior is triggering an unhealed wound or event that happened to us.**

Let's review each one of these.

"They are showing us what we expect."

Yes, quite often we are creating the script in our own minds, and this person is just coming and fulfilling his part. It's like in school when every teacher keeps telling a student that they are "dumb" or "bad." The kid soon believes that they are "dumb" and "bad" and will act that way.

As a former educator, I learned that the greatest predictor of student performance was teacher expectation. The same goes with relationships. A lot of women expect and assume some negative things about men.

For example, a common belief is that all men cheat. Guess what? If you believe all men cheat, every man you date will cheat on you. It is a myth that society perpetuates that men are more sexual than women (highly untrue, and I will discuss this in the following chapter, "Fall in Love With YOU").

The culture we live in leads women to believe that men are naturally unfaithful sex fiends, while women are naturally chaste and monogamous. The fact is both men and women cheat. However, many women automatically start acting suspicious in relationships, checking through their man's phone and text messages, trying to "catch" him cheating. When they find any hint of something, they go nuts and wind up pushing the man away.

Once you are putting that energy out there, the law of attraction is going to bring it to you. As the saying goes,

"When you look for something, you're going to find it!"

Go back and look through your list. Which of those things reflect an expectation that you previously had about how men are? Were you taught as a child that men are not reliable? Did your mother have a distrust of men that you inherited? Be honest, what is your expectation for how men function?

Many of us have extremely low expectations, and our dating experiences reflect that. I know that some women might be thinking, but there *are* men who cheat, who are unreliable and unavailable. Well, that's true. The question is, what in *your* vibration attracted that man to *you*? What are your expectations and beliefs? Where did they come from? Are they even yours? Remember the questions from this poem:

"where did it begin? what went wrong?
and who made you feel so worthless?"

Uncovering Family Wounds

In the case of Larry, I had an expectation that men I really liked would never really want me in return. During the course of our relationship, I was always afraid that he was going to tell me that he didn't want to see me anymore. This was a deep fear, rooted in childhood wounds from my parents.

The majority of our expectations come from deep fears that were implanted in us as children or from early relationships with the opposite sex. In my case, the wound of not feeling wanted came from both my parents. As a child, I experienced my mother as super masculine. As a single mother, raising three kids, going to school at night, working during the day, she had a volatile temper and would often curse and yell at us. I did not receive much affection or soft nurturing from my mother. Because of her own wounds, she was emotionally unavailable.

Not having that emotional support as a child implanted a pattern within me of being attracted to unavailable men. I associated love with lack, being ignored, and shut down. In relationships, I loved men, hoping to convince them of my worthiness to be loved, while at the same time subconsciously reinforcing my own feelings of unworthiness, because these men were not ready to love me.

A major reason why people are unavailable is because they fear being hurt because of some past experience. These people experience an event so traumatic that it causes them to shut off their emotional world to others, because it would be too painful to get hurt again.

My mother did not start telling me she loved me until I was a teenager, due to her own traumatic life. To have a parent like that (especially a mother who was supposed to naturally be more caring, sensitive, and nurturing) can cause deep wounds around love and attachment.

In the case of my father, he was nurturing and caring, but during my early life he had a drug addiction, so he was often physically absent. When my parents got a divorce because of his substance abuse issues, I remember crying because I thought it was "my fault." I thought I had done something "wrong" that caused my father to leave. Therefore, I began to expect the men who I really loved to not be around consistently or not truly be there for me, and that when this happened, it was because something was "wrong" with me.

What was your early relationship like with your parents? Write a paragraph talking about this topic. Did you inherit beliefs and expectations about love from your parents? If so, what were they? Write them down. For example, here are mine:

1. I could not have a loving and emotionally close relationship (mother).

2. Men who I really like and care for won't stay with me because I'm not "good enough" (father).

So, reflecting on my relationship with Larry, I realized, of course, he would "choose" another woman over me because deep down that's what I expected. I expected to be left, not cared for, and rejected. Our patterns are rooted in the relationships we had with one or both of our parents. We learn about love from the ones who were first supposed to love us. This primary relationship shapes our views and expectations about love. These beliefs then play out later in our romantic partnerships and even in our choice of mates.

Please understand that the purpose of this exercise is not to blame our parents. Many of them did the best they could, according to what they knew, and they were in need of their own healing. I do not hold anger at my mother or my father. The traumatic life my mother experienced, honestly, I don't even know if I could have survived it, but I'm thankful that she did. I admire her strength, while acknowledging that she was wounded.

My father has been clean for more than 20 years and is physically present in my life now. I feel blessed to have him. However, though we might understand things about our parents on an intellectual level, these imprints are made at a time when our spirits are impressionable and receptive. In my brain, I was not mad at my mother or my father, but deep down inside I was still carrying the little girl who needed a hug from her mother and wanted her father around.

Go through your list, mark the things your ex did that reflected your expectation based on family wounds or messages about love that you received as a child.

So now that you know what beliefs and expectations your relationship was mirroring back to you, let's move on to the second reason we often feel hurt in relationships:

"They are mirroring back our behavior to us."

I remember when I was married, one of the biggest issues I had with my husband was that he was unmotivated and not goal oriented. I thought he had so much potential but was not utilizing it to his fullest capacity. He wanted to be a doctor but never pursued going to medical school. One day I was complaining to one of my girlfriends about this behavior. I thought I would be better off with a man who was a "go getter" and got things done!

In the same conversation, I told this girlfriend about how I much I wanted to write and perform, but I felt so stuck. I would begin projects and not finish them, and I really wanted to get back on stage after having my son but did not know how. This lovely friend of mine pointed out to me that the reason I was mad at my husband for not fulfilling his potential was because I was not fulfilling mine.

In the same way that he lacked direction for his career, I lacked direction for my art—which was my real passion. At that time, I dismissed her perspective, thinking it was not the same thing. Later on, when I thought about it, I see it was totally the same thing! I had a huge blockage to my creativity during my marriage and after years of being an artist, it really saddened me to be disconnected to something I once loved.

I would remember all the honors and awards I won in high school and think, *What happened to me?* I knew I had great potential, based on my past recognitions, but it was not being expressed. Subconsciously, seeing this similar behavior in my husband really pissed me off, but I did not know why.

Many times, when we get riled up over something our partner does, it's because we do the same thing. The universe is trying to bring this to our attention to help us transform the behavior by showing us what it looks like in another person. Many times, though, we miss the message, because we are too busy pointing the finger and not realizing, as my mother would say, that "our shit also stinks."

Even in the situation of my Larry, I realize I too was unavailable! Shortly before starting to date him, one day I had fervently stated to my girlfriends that I had no desire to be in a relationship. While all my other girlfriends were expressing how much they wanted a partner, I scoffed at them, proclaiming I deeply desired my freedom. After being married, I did not want an "owner."

Well, lo and behold, less than six months later, these words were being echoed right back to me from a dear masculine reflection! He too wanted his freedom, had just left a relationship, and did not want to "settle down." Though, of course, my desire changed during our time together, he still reflected a part of me that was ready to evolve. He helped me change from being unavailable to being available and really wanting a relationship!

Remember how I mentioned that he was involved with another woman? Other than this being something I attracted because of my expectation, it was also a reflection. I was dealing with other men! This relationship was so transformative, because I realized how much of a mirror he was. Once I realized that these patterns no longer suited me, I was ready to make a change.

Sometimes, when we recognize our mirror and decide to evolve, the person will change with us, other times the relationship will end, because we have received the lesson.

Our relationship was no longer tenable for either of us, so it ended.

Please go through your list and mark what behaviors your ex did that reflected things you also did. You might be surprised what you find!

Through dating Larry, I gained more clarity about what I wanted and what I did not want. I also rediscovered my worth and value as a woman. Sometimes as women, when we really want to be with a man, we tolerate behaviors that if anyone else treated us like that, we would chew them out.

This lack of respect for ourselves is then mirrored back, which brings us to the third reason we get upset with our partners:

"They are treating us the way we treat ourselves."

Many times we, as women, don't hold men to a high standard of behavior, because we fear they will leave us. We're bored or lonely and sometimes we tolerate nonsense. I'm sure many of us have witnessed a girlfriend bend over backward for a man who would just use and abuse her in return. We whisper among ourselves that "so-and-so is so stupid!" Sometimes, we are this woman (maybe our friends are reflecting us? Hmmmm . . .).

I can testify that when I was really into a man, I did not hold him accountable for his actions in the same way that I did with men I had no interest in. This demonstrated a lack of respect for myself. So, if I did not treat myself with respect by making my desires, wishes, and standards known, how could the men treat me with respect? The repercussions for this would ultimately be that the men I did not want would chase me more, because they liked the challenge, while the men I liked would violate my boundaries, because I did not respect myself enough to express them.

Ladies, save yourselves the heartache and first honor YOU! Be honest about what you want and what you do not want. When we treat ourselves with love and respect, then men step it up and reflect it back to us in return! In my work with women who are struggling with self-esteem issues, they often attract a man who will mirror that back to them. The man will call them names, tell them how "fat and lazy, " etc., they are. While this behavior, of course, is unacceptable, when I probe deeper, I often find that the hurtful words often reflect how the women feel about themselves.

I've dedicated a WHOLE chapter to loving yourself! Chapter three is all about falling in love with YOU, because this is so, so important!

Go through your list now, and mark the behaviors your ex did that reflected how you felt about or treated yourself.

The last thing we need to look at in our "Mirror, Mirror" exercise is if the behaviors of our ex made us angry because,

**"Their behavior is triggering an
unhealed wound or event that happened to us."**

We talked about family wounds, which are deeply implanted within us during childhood. Sometimes, we also carry wounds from other relationships that we are not conscious of, and when the person we're dating does the same things as an ex, we go ballistic.

For example, I have a friend who hates when anyone "lies" to her. In dating, if she *thinks* she catches a man in a lie, she will completely go off on them, yelling and cursing like a crazy woman. This is due to her prior experience in a marriage, where her husband constantly lied to her. It does not even matter if the person is really lying to her or not, she *perceives* that he is, and it triggers an explosive reaction.

The response the man receives is often way out of proportion with the event that happened. She *over* reacts and is unaware that she is not even responding to the present situation, she is reacting to the past trauma that she has not let go of. She often shouts, "I hate liars!" and talks about how, "All men are big-ass liars!" Which, of course, is only going to bring men who lie to her, because this is what she is focused on.

I'm sure many of us have been the victim of such actions from others. Someone you are dating blows up about something that you thought was not a big deal. They "go off" and leave you standing there thinking, "What in the world was that about?" Most likely, it was not even about you.

In relationships, if we've been hurt in the past, we can often do this. It is the ego's way of trying to protect itself. When the original event that hurt us happened, we went into a state of trance and our spirit became programmed with this trauma. The neurons in our brain got wired to have this kind of response. We have to release it, so that we are no longer a prisoner to our past.

Go through your list one last time, did any of the behaviors of your ex trigger a past traumatic wound or event from a previous relationship? Mark it.

Whew! We just did a lot of work! Give yourself a hug after you complete the "Mirror, Mirror" Soul Work Assignment! If you approached this openly and honestly you should now know exactly how and why you attracted your ex to you. You should see how he was a mirror image of your great potential, your expectations about love, family wounds, past relationships, and your own behaviors. What you just did was **major,** and I guarantee that it will change your life and how you approach dating in the future.

You now stand soul naked in front of your magic mirror, fully empowered with the knowledge that you create your life, ready to let go of all past patterns that no longer serve you. We have dug up a lot of "stuff," so now I'm going to offer some practices to help you heal these wounds and transform yourself, so that the reflections you see in the future represent the love you want and deserve.

Read through the practices and choose the ones that most speak to you. Feel free to do all of them, if that feels right. You might want to take a break before moving on, take some time to process what you discovered. As I suggested, you might want to talk through your findings with a close friend. As always, I'm here for one-on-one coaching.

Here is a little poem that you can use as an affirmation or prayer to help you process your experience with the "Mirror, Mirror" exercise.

I am the caterpillar, cocooning

Naked, stripped

I shed

blisters, skin

What once was

No longer is

I slip off wounds,

Pierce through walls

I fly on silk wings

The past a memory

To fertilize my new beginning

I am free

~~~~~

Soul Work Assignment #5
Letting Go of Family
Agreements and Patterns

Tools: Pen and paper, "Mirror, Mirror" assignment work, white clothing, sacred space, white and/or blue candles, incense

Preparation: In this soul work, we are going to let go of the past patterns we discovered that were planted in us from childhood. Go back to your "Mirror, Mirror" work and find what you wrote about the beliefs and expectations regarding love you inherited from your parents. Did you leave anything out? Along with the behavior they showed you, did they instill any messages in you about men?

We often receive negative messages about men from our mothers or other women in our family. My mother would often tell me that men could not be trusted. Write down a list of the patterns, beliefs, and ideas you received from either your mother or your father. If either parent was absent, what ideas did you deduct about love from their absence? Mine was that men I loved would not stay with me. After this, you might want to take a shower/bath to prepare for the meditation you are going to do. Then do your meditation prep ritual—burn sage, etc.

Meditation: Once you finish your preparation, put on all white clothing and sit in front of your sacred space. Burn a white or blue candle. You might want to place a picture of either your mother or your father on your altar, as you are going to be sending light to their energy. Go through 5–10 minutes of deep breathing. Once you feel relaxed, you are going to imagine two chairs in front of you.

You are going to see your parents, mother and father, coming to sit in front of you in these chairs. When they arrive, thank them for being there to assist you in your healing process.

Tell them that you have inherited some beliefs about love from them that no longer serve you.

Tell them what the beliefs are, and how these expectations have created a pattern in your love life that you are releasing.

Tell them that you hold no anger or grudges against them for the damaging beliefs you inherited.

Tell them that you realize they carried their own pain and were in need of their own healing.

Let them know the work you are doing is for them *and* you; that you desire to have them also feel happy and whole.

Now, turn to each parent and speak the pattern you inherited from them, starting with the words, "I release." For example, I would say to my mother, "I release the belief that I cannot have a caring and emotionally close relationship that I inherited from you. I now proclaim that this pattern no longer has any power over my life." To my father, I would say, "I release the belief that men who I love will not stay with me that I inherited from you. I now proclaim that this pattern no longer has any power over my life."

After you say these statements, see each parent agreeing with you that this pattern no longer has a hold on your life. See them wish you well on your journey and thank you for the great work you're doing that not only benefits your life, but also theirs.

Once they both speak this statement, imagine a brilliant white light crisscrossing between you and them. The light is moving faster and faster and symbolizes this pattern being cut and elevated. See your parents begin to glow also in this light until all that sits before you are two big globes of brilliant light. As the balls of light glow, see them being elevated and getting larger and larger, until they burst in a great explosion. See the light of healing and expansion twinkle all over your skin, you are now also glowing.

As you look out in front of you, where you parents were, there is now a big wide-open road that represents the new possibilities you are going to create in place of the old pattern. See yourself walking down this beautiful, bright road filled with joy. Feel free to explore the beautiful sights you see as you walk along your new path. Once you feel light and complete, you should go to sleep. As always, pay attention to your dreams.

A Note on This Soul Work Assignment: Depending on the nature of the relationship you have/had with your parents, this could be relatively easy or hard. If you suffered serious abuse from either parent and don't feel safe to invite them into your space, that is fine. Instead of imagining them, you can imagine something else that symbolizes the pattern, such as a rock or certain type of animal that personifies what you are letting go of. This meditation can be done, even if a parent is deceased.

Energy is neither created nor destroyed—only transformed; so our loved ones are always with us. They can still hear our requests and feel our intentions. If you find that you are harboring anger toward either parent, then before doing this ritual re-do Soul Assignment #2 by writing a letter to them expressing all you want to say. In this case, you can either burn the letter, or, if you want, speak to your parents directly about how their actions affected you.

It's important that if you choose to speak with your parents, you do it from a place of love and not anger. It's also important that you do it without the expectation to get a certain response. Sometimes, now that our parents are older, they might be more open to sharing with you what was going on with them, and why they did what they did. Other parents will immediately jump to the defensive and make you feel even worse. So again, their response is not important.

Of course, you do not need to speak to them at all, if you don't wish to. You can burn the letter after you write it, and trust that your intention is being transmuted and complete your release with the above meditation. What you might find happens after the meditation is that during the course of an ordinary conversation with your parents, some of the topics you wrote about might naturally come up. If so, allow it, it could be healing for both of you.

Soul Work Assignment #6
Re-Patterning Meditation

Tools: Pen and paper, "Mirror, Mirror" Soul Work Assignment, white clothes, white and/or blue candle

Preparation: Go through your "Mirror, Mirror" work and identify any specific traumatic or hurtful experiences or events that you identified as creating a pattern in your life that needs healing. For example, my friend who is reacting negatively to men she thinks are lying to her would go back and find a scenario in which her ex-husband was lying. Find an event that really represents the pattern you are releasing. This could be a situation with your parents, family members, or an ex-lover. You might want to choose up to three to work on and perform this meditation for each. In your meditation, you are going to go back and re-pattern this event. Do your meditation preparations.

Meditation: In front of your sacred space, begin breathing deeply for 5–10 minutes. Once you get to a state of relaxation, recreate the scenario just as you experienced it in your mind. Try to imagine it as vividly as possible, use your five senses.

Where were you, when it happened?

What did the room look like?

What did it smell like?

Who was there?

Were you eating anything?

What did the food taste like?

Do you remember what anyone was wearing?

How did you feel?

See it as clearly as possible. If this is too painful to do, then you might want to imagine a symbol of strength and protection in the room with you. This could be an angel, religious figure, or deity you feel connected to. It could even be your grandmother. Know that this being is here to protect you and help you heal this event.

As you see the situation play out, see how you reacted originally. You might have cried, maybe you walked away, perhaps you did not say anything and pretended that everything was all right.

After you visualize this, then you are going to see yourself saying to the person or persons, "No, this is not how this goes." You might want to bring your angel or being of protection closer to you. Once you feel the power, then you are going to say everything you *wish* you could have said in this situation. Whatever it is you want to say to this person, let them have it. Release your truth about how their actions made you feel and how unacceptable it is.

Once you feel confident that you have released enough verbally, see this person being receptive to what you had to say. Visualize them reacting the way you want them to react, it's all up to you. You might want them to hug you and tell you that you're beautiful and they love you. You might just want them to leave and never come back. Maybe the deity or religious figure takes them away from you.

After you're finished with them, feel a warm light embracing you. It might even be your angel or your ancestors. Know that you have the help and power of the universe to aid you in your healing. Feel a great love surrounding you and supporting your release of this pattern. Receive that you are free and no longer controlled by the past.

A Note on This Soul Work Assignment: As with the previous meditation, this one is powerful and will probably get emotional for you. It's okay to cry and feel the release. We are shifting major patterns that are affecting your life and years of pain. You might be surprised about how much you actually remember about this event, once you recall it in a state of trance. I've had visions while doing this that were so clear—it was shocking.

I would remember the specific pajamas I wore as a child or what color the carpet was when I was seven years old, things I had not thought about in years. Also, when you imagine them saying what you would want them to say, you don't need to slip into the logical brain and think "Oh, that person would never say or do that, why am I deluding myself?"

As a theater student at NYU, while prepping for scene work, I was taught that the mind does not know the difference between what is imagined and what is real. Before performing a character for a scene, my acting teacher would have me perform the scene in my mind first. When one imagines something, the brain will start firing off the same signals and responses, as if the event was actually happening.

We are working on rewiring our brains, so that we are no longer attached to negative experiences in our past. While doing this meditation, you are reconnecting synapses in your brain to create a different pattern in your life—one in which you can speak your truth, and your feelings are honored and protected.

Soul Work Assignment #7
Get Light Ritual

Tools: "Mirror, Mirror" assignment, rocks, a bag, a body of water (river, lake, or ocean)

Preparation: Go through your "Mirror, Mirror" assignment one last time and make a list of every pattern, situation, and behavior you want released. If you've found that your past partners have been mirroring back to you behaviors you no longer wish to embody, write them down.

Once you have your list, you're going to go out into nature, find a nearby park, and choose a rock that symbolizes each thing you want to release. If your list has ten things, then you should have ten rocks. If some of the things on your list represent big patterns or were situations that had a large impact on you, then you might choose a large rock that symbolically represents the magnitude of this event or pattern. After you gather all your rocks, put them in a bag.

Ritual

The day that you choose to do this, you're going to start in the morning with carrying around the rocks that represent your wounds and patterns. Take these rocks, all day, wherever you go. Know that the heaviness you feel represents how these scars are weighing you down.

At sundown, go to a river, lake, or ocean. You might wish to take a sister friend with you to support you, or you might go alone, if you feel safe. As you stand at the water's edge, say a prayer to the higher power you believe in. You might also ask your ancestors to be present as you are also doing this healing work for them.

Tell Spirit, your ancestors, and your guides what your intentions are. Ask them to give you the strength and the power to release these wounds that are weighing you down.

Ask the energy of the water to help you by taking these wounds, as represented by these rocks, and use its ancient sacred properties to heal them. Water is a major element used in healing and cleansing around the world. Our bodies are greatly connected to this, as we are mostly water and can easily tap into this element for our healing work.

After you say your prayers, you are going to take each rock, one by one, and throw it into the water. You might want to have the list you compiled nearby to use as a reference for each pattern/wound you're releasing. You might also wish to memorize the list or know it well enough so that you are saying each thing you are releasing as you toss each rock in the water.

Your release statement can go like this,

"I release all the ways this (emotion, belief, event, pattern) is affecting my life. I now proclaim myself free of this."

You might say this silently in your head or out loud to yourself. If you have a sister there to support you, ask her to witness your ritual and offer words of encouragement, as you are making a major shift in your life.

Once you finish releasing all your old patterns and wounds into the water, thank the energy of the water for its healing and transformative power. You might even want to leave some flowers by the side of the water as an offering. Thank God and your ancestors for being present with you and ask them to give you the power not to pick up these wounds and patterns again.

As you walk away from the water, you should feel light, you might want to sing or listen to an inspirational song, as you have just done some major healing work.

Take a shower or bath when you get home, put on your whites, and quietly spend your evening. Be gentle with yourself during the next few days and write down any feelings, dreams, thoughts, or insights that come to you.

A Note on This Soul Work Assignment: We have just completed some incredible healing in this chapter! You should be proud of yourself, because not everyone is ready to do this work! Many people spend years blaming others for their misery, not realizing that life is their mirror, nor do they have the tools to get themselves free. Other people are in fact imprisoned by their stories and addicted to their pains. You, my dear, are not one of those people!

The work you did is miraculous, and I guarantee that if you did it with an honest, open heart and good intentions, you will watch your life transform before your eyes. This does not mean, however, that everything will be perfect, or that you'll never ever again feel the wounds or patterns you released. They might try to creep back in, but they gain strength from the energy you give them.

As a plant ceases to grow, once you stop watering it, your old wounds and patterns will do the same, if you don't energize them by repeating your behaviors. Feel free to repeat any of the Soul Work Assignments, if something new comes up. These are your tools to heal yourself!

Take your time with this, always being sweet and gentle with yourself. You are amazing, and you deserve to be free of the pain of the past! You are powerful and entitled to a life of peace, joy, and bliss! Now that we have cleared out those things we no longer need, let's fill up with the ecstasy of self-love!

Items Needed for
Chapter 3
Fall in Love with YOU

- ✓ Bubble bath soap or fragrant bath salts

- ✓ Yellow and pink candles

- ✓ Natural massage oil (almond, coconut, grapeseed oil, etc.)

- ✓ Jade egg

- ✓ Sea salt

- ✓ Pink flowers

- ✓ ½ gallon milk (cow or goat)

- ✓ Handheld mirror

- ✓ Sweet-smelling oils or perfume (rose, sandalwood, or orange oil recommended)

- ✓ **Optional**: Flowers, wine, champagne, or sparkling cider

Chapter 3
Fall in Love with YOU

"First become alone. First start enjoying yourself.
First love yourself. First become so authentically happy that
if nobody comes it doesn't matter;
you are full, overflowing.
If nobody knocks at your door it is perfectly ok—
YOU are not missing.
You are not waiting for somebody to
come and knock at the door.
You are at home.
If somebody comes, good, beautiful.
If nobody comes, that too is beautiful and good."

—Osho

It was a golden summer day. Pink, yellow, and purple flowers sashayed in the breeze. The air was warmed by the kiss of the sun. That's when I saw her, skin a melody of rich brown, hair projecting out a black halo. She must be an angel, but she wasn't the image of any angels I had ever seen—porcelain-looking creatures with rosy cheeks and Rapunzel hair. She was like Angela Davis, dancing in the sacred river waters of the Nile. She was the revolution draped in rose-colored satin wearing a gardenia in her hair.

This woman seemed to be so completely at peace and in love with herself that everyone stopped to notice. Women who passed by gave her a nod of sisterhood. Men were arrested by the sight of her and couldn't help but utter,

"Good morning, beautiful." She wasn't the image of what *Vogue* or even the latest music videos portrayed as "beauty," her wide nose and kinky hair, once symbols of oppression, were now signs of pride. She was a woman completely smacked with joy, exhilarated by living in her own skin.

As I watched her, I began to notice this woman was slightly familiar. There was something in her smile that I connected with. As I passed a store window, I caught my image, almost stopped in my tracks. I realized this woman was me . . .

~~~~~

When we start doing the really beautiful work of falling in love with ourselves, we often experience ourselves as a surprise. Throughout most of my life, if you had asked me if I loved myself, I would have told you yes. Perhaps mostly that would have been true. But the reasons *why* I thought I loved myself at 20, and the reasons I do now, are completely different. In my twenties, I probably loved myself based on things outside myself—because I had a degree and was really smart. I had a good job and could financially take care of myself. Maybe I thought I was kind of cute 'cause some guy had paid me attention. None of these things had anything to do with who I was inside as a woman. For the most part, I was still trying to locate happiness inside a man who could "complete" me.

I experienced a lot of rollercoaster emotions around dating. If some dude I really liked wanted me, I felt happy. If he didn't, I felt dejected and alone. However, for the past several years I have been on a radical journey to learn how to first fall in love with myself.

I have learned how to make myself happy, no matter what anyone else does or does not do. The joy and complete bliss that I've found within myself cannot be compared to anything else. At one time, if I was by myself on a Saturday night, I felt like a loser. Now, if I am alone, I relish the sacredness of my own presence. This has taken a lot of work, but I will not lie, the journey has been fun and, dare I say, orgasmic!

A lot of times, we women can be like that grandma with the beautiful, but dusty, china dinnerware sitting in our closets, waiting for the moment that "special" dinner guest arrives for a visit. Well, I'm here to tell you to dust off those plates, bring out the champagne flutes, and pop that bottle because that special guest is here, the special one you've been waiting for is YOU!

Now that we've cleared some major patterns and false beliefs, we are stepping into the truth of who we are and we are going to love, love, love ourselves! I'm going to share some practices that I discovered that have awakened my own inner goddess and helped me experience more pleasure, joy, and self-love than ever before. We are going to begin with something most women struggle with—our body image.

Loving Our Bodies as Temples of the Soul

"If tomorrow, women woke up and decided they really liked their bodies, just think how many industries would go out of business."

— Dr. Gail Dines

Many industries are fattening their bank accounts from the self-hate of women. Reality TV is riddled with exposés of people getting plastic surgery, whether it's a nose job, tummy tuck, or breast implants. While some folks might get a little nip and tuck here and there, others come out much worse than how they started.

In a story published in *Essence* magazine in November 2012, a woman lost both her arms and legs due to illegal butt injections. Wherever women turn, it seems someone is telling us that we are too fat or too skinny, butt too big or not big enough. The plastic surgery and cosmetic industry is a multimillion dollar business that often preys on the shattered self-esteem of women. In the words of Beyoncé, far too often, "pretty hurts."

Much of the work that needs to be done in regard to self-love is deeply connected to us loving our bodies and the way we look. Many of us experience wounding from childhood, sometimes from our own family members. I will never forget the day in sixth grade that I was called ugly. I was a student at Turner Junior High, my neighborhood school that was like a scene out of the film *Dangerous Minds*. Many kids did not care two cents about their education, openly disrespected teachers, and fought among themselves due to their own feelings of powerlessness. My best friend in the sixth grade had her ponytail set on fire, and my class locked the math teacher out of her own classroom while they trashed it.

Now we all know middle school is the crux of awkwardness, and here I was, a tall, shy, nerdy girl from the 'hood who liked to read books. I stuck out like a nun in a strip club. When I was twelve, two of my "friends" thought it would be funny to write letters to this boy named Kevin, who they thought I liked. Truthfully, I wanted *nothing* to do with Kevin, and the girls probably knew that, but just thought forging love notes in my name would be funny (middle school girls can be so cruel).

They wrote him three letters, supposedly from me, saying how much I liked him. One day, while heading to gym, our class was walking down the staircase at the same time as Kevin's class. My so-called "friends" started pushing us together saying, "There goes your man!"

In the sea of pimply, middle school children, I tried to raise my voice to tell him, "No, I didn't write the letters!" But he did not hear me. Instead, the entire sixth grade class and I heard him as he said, "I don't like you! You UGLY!" His words were like a bucket of ice water thrown on my face. The whole class broke into laughter on the staircase, and my soul slinked back into a corner and cried. The next three days I became "sick" and stayed home from school.

Most of us have a story about someone doing something to us that makes our soul slink back in a corner feeling "ugly" and ashamed. (I have done a "Re-Patterning" Meditation on this event, and I encourage you to re-pattern any trauma you encountered dealing with beauty or body image).

TLC had a song that called it feeling, "unpretty." Though we might grow up and become successful—with a good job, house, and car—many of us still struggle day to day with feelings of low self-esteem. This lack of self-love only gets exacerbated in relationships.

I believe, as women, most of us don't know how beautiful we actually are. I use the word "beautiful" on purpose. I believe that there are women who think they are "cute" or "pretty" but not necessarily BEAUTIFUL. The beauty I am speaking of is not so much about your physical qualities but more about an inner, vibrant light that shines from your whole being that everyone can feel around you. This inner light, this inner beauty, is not only a blessing to you, it is a blessing to all those you encounter.

To quote actress Jane Seymour,

"Beauty is a radiance that originates from within and comes from inner security and strong character."

I would also add that beauty comes from a deep bliss that is bubbling inside you until it becomes a tangible energy that overflows. This bliss for me comes from loving myself.

When I speak of loving one's self, I am not talking about the ego, which pumps itself up based on false identifications. Like I mentioned before, our ego seeks an identity with changeable things outside itself, such as money, relationships, cars, education, physical looks, etc. All these things will come and go, as the only thing constant is change. We must locate our happiness and our beauty within our higher selves. This higher self is already complete and whole. The nature of our higher self is peace and love, and it is an eternal never-changing state. In the sacred words of the ancient Bhagavad Gita,

> *"These bodies come to an end;*
> *but that vast embodied Self*
> *is ageless, fathomless, eternal."*

From this ageless, fathomless, and eternal part of us is where our true beauty shines. Let me be clear, because I do not want to create a higher self vs. a lower self dichotomy. There are some pseudo-religious leaders who will make you feel guilty for experiencing any so-called "negative" emotion or "sin." Many people feel pressured to strive for this mythical image of perfection that floats on gluten-free clouds above all desire and worldly connections.

I believe EVERY part of me is holy! I embrace my darkness as well as my light. It is through darkness that we rebirth ourselves and are born anew into the light. So, when I speak of beauty shining from our higher selves, it is a self who is a perfect witness to our joy and pain and cherishes us anyway! It is a self not based on material things, but instead on our divine birthright of joy, peace, and love.

As we heal from past relationships and open up to receive a better reflection of love, we must first reflect this love within ourselves. We cannot expect another person to love us the way we deserve to be loved, if we do not first love ourselves this way. As the Osho quote states at the opening of this chapter,

> *"First become alone.*
> *First start enjoying yourself.*
> *First love yourself."*

This entire chapter is filled with juicy goodness that helps you unlock this great love waiting to flow all through and out of you.

Many of us feel we have to pile on makeup or wear uncomfortable high-heel shoes to "get" a man. I have found that in the moments when I'm not "trying" to be beautiful or sexy is when I radiate the most. It is also often when I attract the most positive attention from people. These are times when I'm just going along, minding my business. and I notice the extended glances from men, or I get women asking me about my hair. There used to be a time when a man would approach, and I'd think, "Why is he trying to talk to me? I look a mess!" but now I embrace it.

I realize it is not about how I "look," but something within me that shines and attracts people. It also does not reflect what "society" projects women must do to be considered beautiful. It is in those moments when my hair is big and nappy, when the only thing on my face is almond oil, and my skirt is loose and flowing in the wind, that my beauty shines the most. This is when the world reflects back to me, "Yes, indeed, woman, you are radiant just as you are! The higher self in me bows to the higher self in you!"

So, let's get started with our first Sacred Self Assignment. We are going to begin with the body. As I stated before, many of us hold a negative self-image around our looks, due to past wounds. Though we know the body is temporary, while the self is eternal, it is our home and our temple while here on earth. To quote master Tantric teacher Osho again,

"The first thing is to learn respect for the body,
to unlearn all the nonsense
that has been taught to you about the body.
Otherwise you will never turn on,
and you will never turn in,
and you will never turn beyond."

Within the Ifá spiritual tradition, originating from the Yoruba people in Nigeria (known also in Cuba as Santería or Lucumí and in Brazil as Candomblé), there exists within the spiritual pantheon a goddess called Oshun. She is the patron deity of love, femininity, sensuality, beauty, friendship, harmony, wealth, and fertility. She is a great healer, especially of women. She is associated with rivers, honey, the color yellow, brass, and the number five.

In my work with Oshun, she has taught me to truly love myself in every single way. The following practice is inspired by her. For me, Oshun represents the aspect of God's consciousness where we come into the body and begin to celebrate our physical form as a temple of the Divine. In the Hindu Tantric tradition, she can be linked with the second chakra, Svadhisthana, which means "sacred home of the self."

As we tap into our sensuality, it is really us opening up to feel the rush of the Divine through our physical form and senses. We are celebrating our bodies as that which houses our sacred spirits and is blessed enough to experience the sweetness of life. Every single time we experience pleasure, we are opening up to the ecstasy of being alive. The fact that we are alive is an absolute miracle. So we love our bodies, not because we're "cute," but because at our core we are pure BEAUTY and LOVE that celebrates its right to exist. Let us always remember,

"You are liquid love in physical bodies,
wanting, more than life itself,
because it is life itself, to adore the vessel
that's you through which this
Source Energy flows.
You are God. You are Source. You are creator."

—Abraham

Sacred Self Assignment #1
Love Your Body

Tools: Bubble bath soap or fragrant bath salts. Yellow and pink candles. Massage oil. A full-length mirror.

Optional: Flowers, wine, champagne or sparkling cider, incense.

Preparation: Gather all items needed for this ritual and select a nice quiet evening. (Friday evenings are perfect for this assignment.)

Ritual

1. Take a nice, luxurious bath. You can add bubbles, bath salts, or scented oils to accent the water. Light pink and yellow candles, and burn a sensual incense. My favorite to burn is sandalwood. The more elements you add that make you feel soft and beautiful, the better! Soak in the bath for at least 30 minutes, while listening to soft, sensual music.

2.Once finished bathing, slowly oil up (it's best to use a natural oil, such as coconut oil or almond oil), paying attention to every part of your body as you do. Bless your body. Say out loud, "I bless my feet. I bless my arms. I bless my fingers . . ." etc. You can also wave the incense over your body, paying special attention to your spiritual gates, as mentioned before.

3.When you finish oiling, stand naked and glistening in front of the mirror—a full-length mirror is best. As you stand before your beautiful body, tell yourself that you love yourself. Then take your time and tell every body part what you love about it. Example: "I love how wide and juicy my hips are. I love the gap between my teeth." Etc.

4.Try to give love especially to those parts that you have neglected or feel shame about. It is important to love ALL of you, if you expect anyone else to.

5.When you finish, give yourself a hug. Allow tears or whatever needs to happen during this exercise. Spend the evening doing something that makes you feel happy, sipping wine, watching your favorite movie (something light, funny, or romantic), reading passages of poetry, etc.

A Note on This Soul Work Assignment: After completing the "Love Your Body" Sacred Self Assignment, begin to notice your "self talk." Do you spend a lot of time judging, criticizing, and cursing yourself? Is your reflex to look in the mirror and notice what is "wrong" with you? Now, no need to become obsessive and start counting how many times you talk down to yourself, but just see if you can bring a gentle awareness to your patterns of thought.

Work on talking to yourself and your body in loving ways every day. As author and speaker Dr. Steve Maraboli said,

"There is nothing more rare, nor more beautiful than a woman being unapologetically herself; comfortable in her perfect imperfection. To me that is the essence of beauty."

It is our "imperfections" that make us unique and beautiful. Love ALL of you!

Now that we have begun with an overall appreciation of our bodies, we are going to delve even deeper into not only loving ourselves, but sending healing energy to our feminine organs, while expanding our level of orgasmic bliss. Oh, yes! It's about to get sexy and fun!

Reclaiming Our Sexual Organs and Our Right to Ecstasy

The first time I had an orgasm, I was four years old. I did not know what it was, of course, all I knew was that touching "down there" felt good, and I enjoyed it. As I began to receive messages from my family and society, I learned that touching "down there" was wrong, and I began to feel guilty. I thought I was "dirty" if I touched myself. Masturbating became the thing I did in the dark, under the sheets, but felt bad about.

From the time many of us are young girls, we grow up with negative feelings attached to our sexual organs. We might have noticed that touching ourselves feels good, but had a well-meaning parent shoo our hand away or tell us it was wrong. Often times within our subconscious, we carry the idea that our genitals are "nasty." For women, this can become especially pronounced as we move through adolescence and begin menstruating and feel shame around our sacred fluid. If there was sexual abuse or trauma, connecting to our sexuality in a healthy way can be particularly challenging.

In this section, we are going to journey into a self-love that includes having a positive relationship with our breasts and yoni (ancient Sanskrit word for vagina, meaning "divine passage" or "sacred temple"). We are going to learn how to make love to OURSELVES! While I won't be giving a blow-by-blow explanation about how to masturbate, I will be showing you some ancient techniques that women have used for thousands of years to maintain their health and also connect in a positive way to their sexuality. We are going to take that which has been used to shame us, and reclaim it to empower us!

Bow Down!

In the Hindu Tantric system the yoni was worshipped as a symbol of the goddess and recognized as the divine pathway of life. Images of the yoni were carved into temple walls and molded into sacred relics. The ancients did not have the Internet, but they were connected to the divine energy pulsing through the matrix of life. Our precious yoni flowers are sacred, period (pun intended). It is time to put our yonis back on the throne! It does not matter what your yoni has been through—neglect, abuse, abortion, STDs, etc.— she is worthy of worship! In this next process, we are going to connect to our yoni and elevate her to her rightful status as holy and beautiful.

Sacred Self Assignment #2
Yoni Speaks

Tools: Paper and pen

Preparation: Meditation preparations. Dress comfortably, skirt or dress suggested.

Meditation: Close your eyes and practice deep breathing for a few minutes until you feel relaxed. As you continue your breathing, you're going to focus on breathing into your yoni. This might sound weird, but imagine when you are breathing, you are breathing deep down into your yoni. You can even play with the idea that on the in breath as the breath drops down, the yoni expands, and on the out breath, she relaxes. You might start to notice as you breathe that a light sensation of pleasure warms you, if that happens, allow it. Know that your yoni was designed to experience pleasure. (It is a known fact that the clitoris has twice as many nerve endings as the penis. More nerve endings means more ability to feel sensation.)

Continue to breathe into the yoni for a few minutes. When you feel ready, see if you can, in your imagination, travel to your yoni. See what she looks like with your inner eye. Allow yourself to explore the idea of seeing into the inner world of your yoni. What you see might be quite literal—soft, silky pink walls or more symbolic. Perhaps you see your yoni as a warm, blue ocean in the Caribbean or a soft, playful kitten.

When you get an image of your yoni, ask her to speak to you. Ask her what she would like to say. Tell her she deserves to have a voice, and now it is her time to speak. As you listen to your yoni speak, pay attention to what she says.

What has she been holding back that she needs to express?

What is her personality like?

Is she shy and timid?

Perhaps she is boisterous and outspoken?

Allow her, without judgment, to be whatever she is and say whatever she needs to say. When she finishes, thank her, and let her know that you honor her and love her and promise to make sure that anyone who is blessed enough to meet her will also honor her. When you finish and open your eyes, write down what your yoni had to say.

A Note on This Sacred Self Assignment: The "Yoni Speaks" exercise is a great way to practice being connected to your sexuality. So many times, we only experience our sexuality as reflected back to us from another. Our vaginas are playgrounds for someone else's fantasies, sometimes even for a person who does not deserve to be there. Too often, women experience lovers who do not know how to approach the yoni or please her.

Many women do not even think about their yonis, unless they are being sexually intimate or during their menstrual cycle. But if we want someone else to treat our yonis with care and respect, we must approach her in the same way. We must recognize her as the sacred passageway to life—whether or not you have children.

The opening we, as women, have between our legs allows us to have a powerful connection to the Divine Feminine— the aspect of divinity that is nurturing and receptive. This aspect of our divinity is infinitely creative, not to just create babies—which is a miracle in itself—but also to create what we want in our lives.

After completing this exercise, place your hands on your yoni and crown her the queen goddess she is! Tell her that she is beautiful and worthy of a deep, satisfying love, and the love begins with you. Thank her for her tremendous capacity to experience pleasure and ask that divine light fill your yoni with love.

A Sacred Practice: Breast Massage

As we journey through cultivating and nourishing our sexual energy, we must pay homage to our sacred breasts. There is a connection between our breasts and wombs; breastfeeding moms know this. Nursing a newborn baby stimulates the release of the hormone oxytocin, which causes contractions that help the uterus shrink to its normal size. In the Taoist system of sexual alchemy, breast massage is encouraged as a daily practice to heal the feminine organs and become more sensitive to sexual energy.

While men represent masculine or active energy, and women represent receptive or feminine energy, within our own being there is a masculine and feminine energy dynamic. Within women, the breasts are connected to our heart chakra and are considered our positive or active pole. This is the place we give from energetically.

Our yoni is considered our negative or receptive pole, because it is where we receive. For men, it is the opposite, their penis is the location of their positive pole, where they give and their heart is the location of their negative pole, where they receive. When these energy centers are connected in sacred sexual lovemaking, a beautiful circulation of life force happens. While the discussion of that is beyond the scope of this book, we can harmonize our own energy centers within by connecting to our breasts, the positive pole.

Just like the yoni, many women might carry emotions around their breasts that could range from love, hate, or ambivalence. Maybe you think they are too small and wish they were bigger, or you might have struggled with feeling less of a woman because of your breast size. Perhaps you have big, full breasts and had to deal with men over-sexualizing you.

I know many women who developed early and wanted to hide their breasts as the groping eyes of grown men made them feel embarrassed and uncomfortable. You might not have any emotional charge around your breasts whatsoever and only think about them when you put on your bra in the morning and take it off after work. Whatever your breast story is, we are going to deliberately cultivate having a sensual loving connection to them.

To quote Diana Richardson, in her book *Tantric Orgasm for Women,*

"The breasts have the power to bring woman to the deepest of orgasmic experiences. The breasts are central to a woman's experience of sexual ecstasy" (p. 53).

When we open this energy center, we begin to radiate a confident and soft nurturing energy no matter the size or shape of our breasts. We also open to the expansion of our own orgasmic bliss.

We need to touch our breasts on a regular basis. We give of our breasts to nourish our children and please our lovers, but often we do not spend time enjoying our breasts for ourselves. In the next Sacred Self Assignment, we are going to give ourselves a breast massage, which not only feels good, but is healing to our reproductive organs. Doing a breast massage on a regular basis has many benefits including:

- Naturally increasing your estrogen levels (this helps manage and balance emotions and improve the skin)

- Activating your qi (pronounced chi) or life force energy

- Eliminating lumps or cysts in breasts

- Increasing sensitivity in breasts, making them more orgasmic

- Making breasts fuller

- Stopping or shortening your menstrual cycle, makes it less heavy and painful

- Making your yoni tighter, wetter, and more flexible

- Bringing you into sensual self love

It is such a powerful practice to touch your breasts on a regular basis with loving intentions instead of fear. Many women only actively touch their breasts if they are checking for cancerous tumors. Imagine the energetic imprint it causes when you only touch yourself in fear that something might be wrong. We also cage our breasts in bras. There are many healing reflexology zones in the breasts that become desensitized because our breasts are smashed inside bras for "support."

It is not a coincidence that in cultures where women don't wear bras, their breast cancer rate is the same as men, dramatically lower than countries where women wear bras practically all day long (see *Dressed to Kill: The Link between Breast Cancer and Bras* by Sydney Ross Singer and Soma Grismaijer). Wearing a bra inhibits the proper function of the lymphatic system that is responsible for moving waste out of our bodies. These toxins are unable to move out of the body and then buildup in the tissues of the breasts. (I also recommend that women wear natural deodorants, which do not contain aluminum or other toxic substances).

So, while you do not necessarily need to go and burn your bras, you can become mindful of how long you wear them and perform a breast massage on a regular basis to aid your lymphatic system in flushing out the toxins. Once you become consistent with this practice, you will also notice a difference in your menstrual cycle. When I massage my breasts daily, I practically eliminate all premenstrual symptoms. I won't even know my cycle is coming on until the bleeding starts.

The breast will also become more sensitive to sensations and pleasure. Did you know that there is such a thing as a breast orgasm? Yes! We can have orgasms all over our body, including our breasts. When we connect to our breasts, we also connect to our hearts. Our heart chakra governs our ability to give and receive love. The more we open our hearts to give love, the more love will be reflected back to us in return. Let's start with radiating this love to ourselves first.

Sacred Self Assignment #3
Breast Massage

Tools: Your loving hands

Optional: Natural massage or body oil

Ritual

1. Choose a time when you can do a massage every day, so you can be consistent. I like to do my breast massage in the morning when I get out of the shower as I'm oiling my body, but it can be done anytime, or twice a day, morning and night.

2. Stimulate your sexual energy. This can be done by performing kegels or vaginal contractions to get the energy flowing. You can also sit with a rolled-up sock or ball against your clitoris to keep it stimulated.

3. Rub your hands together to warm them and stimulate the healing energy coming from the meridians in your hands.

4. Place your hands on your breasts and begin rubbing them in outward circles starting around the nipples and moving in a circular motion over the entire breast. Do this a minimum of 24 times and a maximum of 360. (Taoists like to do things in multiples of 9, so you can do 27, 36, 45, etc.) You can also reverse the motion and perform the massage with circles going inward. You should do the outward circle, if your breasts have lumps or cysts. This will help to break up the stagnate energy. Of course, if you notice anything that alarms you, please check with a medical professional.

5. When finished, place your hands on your breasts and imagine a loving green or pink energy shining out from your heart. Take notice of how you feel day to day. You might begin to feel a warm, sweet sexual energy circulating in your breast and heart center as it becomes more open. Take note of any changes in your menstrual cycle.

Initiation into Sexual Kung Fu

Imagine it is the year AD 1200. You are a queen in the royal palace of China. Wearing a beautiful, turquoise, silk gown, you sit in your bedroom quarters ready to retire for the night. Before you do, you perform a ritual that only a select few know about. You take out a scarlet sachet. Inside of it is one of your most beloved secrets, a sacred stone egg made out of jade. As a young princess, you heard about the sacred jade egg and its power. It is rumored to be made from the crystallized essence of dragons.

As a woman, having given birth to three children, it is now your time to experience the magic of the jade egg. You disrobe, holding the egg in your hand. Then you breathe deeply, and insert it into your sensual succulence. You know that this practice is what keeps you looking and feeling youthful. You make love with the dexterity of a woman half your age, and your orgasms shoot you into the heavens. You go to sleep with the mystical stone nestled inside you, with a gentle smile on your face as you drift off into sweet dreams.

The jade egg has become popular in recent years, as many women seek to reclaim their sexual power. As the above anecdote illustrates, its origins are ancient. A practice that was once reserved for the queen and concubines of the royal court in China, the jade egg is now gaining worldwide New Age popularity.

As we journey through healing our hearts and opening to experiencing the love we deserve, I'd like to initiate you into this art of sexual kung fu. Whether you're brand new to the egg or have been using it for a while, I ask that you approach this section with an open mind. Let's explore this magical practice.

What Is a Jade Egg?

A jade egg is a small stone made of jade and cut into the shape of an egg. The egg is inserted into the vagina and used to perform kegel exercises or vaginal kung fu. The egg usually has holes drilled into one of the ends where floss or string is looped through for easy removal from the vagina. Since antiquity, jade as a gemstone has been held in high regard in Chinese culture. It symbolizes wealth and promotes the positive flow of qi or life force energy.

The quality of our life force dictates how healthy and vibrant we are. Taoists in China recognized jade for its tremendous healing abilities, as it contains minerals that are beneficial for the body. Energetically speaking, jade helps women to cultivate yin or feminine qualities; it heals the heart chakra and opens us to love. Jade is also a dream stone that can help promote healing dreams and sleep.

I first discovered the jade egg seven years ago at a belly dance conference shortly after the separation from my husband. It was the first time I had ever heard of the jade egg. I was delighted when I was taught the ancient methods of sexual energy cultivation. The instructor told us that the first time we insert the jade egg, it might fall out, as our muscles might not be strong enough to hold it in.

I remember buying my jade egg and being so excited that I went right back to my hotel room to try it out. After cleaning it, I stood panty-less on top of the hotel bed, as the instructor recommended, in case the egg fell out, so it wouldn't break on the floor. I gently slid the egg in. I felt a slight tinge of apprehension mixed with the excitement of exploring something new. I tried my best to remember the vaginal exercises I learned in class. *Squeeze, squeeze, squeeze! Plop!* The egg landed on my bed. While it might have only stayed in for a few minutes, I was so happy to be opening the gate to my sexual power.

Years later, I have gained more mastery over my muscles; now I can comfortably keep my egg in all day. Sometimes I use two eggs. I also have many different stones. My favorites include rose quartz and obsidian. Each stone has its own benefits, but jade is considered the best stone to begin with because of its gentle healing energy. I can't tell you how sweet it is to be able to practice my sexual kung fu secretly while riding the train, walking down the street, or sitting in a restaurant. It is a secret that only my yoni and I share.

One of my favorite times to practice is while making dinner. I put on a favorite reggae song, and it's a party! There are times that I forget my egg is in, and I find myself swimming in a pool of soft, seductive, sensual energy. I'll start to wonder why I feel so sexual all of a sudden, then remember, yes! I'm wearing an egg!

One of the beautiful things about the jade egg practice is that you do not even have to consciously do the exercises all the time to receive the benefits. You could put the egg in and forget about it all day and still receive its healing energy, your muscles automatically become activated by keeping the egg inside. There are reflexology points in the vagina that connect to other organs in the body. When the egg is inside the vaginal canal, it gently massages the different areas of the yoni, bringing healing energy to the kidneys, liver, spleen, lungs, and heart.

When we add kegels to this practice, it has a powerful effect. While doing kegels has become popular in Western society, especially after women give birth to help strengthen the pelvic floor muscles, when you add a jade egg, it becomes vaginal weight lifting. Imagine you are training to be a body builder and you never use weights, you will never get any results. You must add weight training to build up resistance, which will cause the muscles to get stronger. This is what the jade egg does. It gives your yoni an opportunity to increase her strength, through activating the voluntary and involuntary muscles.

Using the jade egg on a regular basis will also make your yoni more sensitive, which will make sex more pleasurable and increase the chances of experiencing deeper vaginal orgasms as opposed to just clitoral orgasms (yes, love, there are many different kinds of orgasms)! Many women have reported going from non-orgasmic to having multiple orgasms after consistent jade-egg practice. Here is a breakdown of the many benefits of using the jade egg:

- Increases flow of sexual hormones

- Can help prevent or eliminate fibroids

- Breaks up stagnant energy or qi, which leads to disease in the yoni

- Eases discomforts, such as cramps associated with the menstrual cycle (note you cannot use the egg when on your cycle)

- Tones, tightens, and strengthens the yoni by assisting in gaining control of the muscles

- Aids in the natural increase of vaginal fluids, making sex feel better

- Strengthens the pelvic floors muscles, which helps protect against incontinence and pelvic prolapse

- Naturally increases the libido

- Rejuvenates sexual organs

- Prepares for and provides healing from childbirth

Using the jade egg is also completely safe. No need to be afraid it will "get stuck." The egg cannot go beyond the cervix, the opening to our uterus. If you use non-minty floss looped and knotted through the hole in the egg, you can remove it with ease.

For the next Sacred Self Assignment, we are going to add the sacred rites of the mystical jade egg to honor and heal the yoni. Please note this is a powerful practice, but you will only get results through using it consistently. You might experience a surge in your sexual energy after use. This can be exhilarating. But remember to be mindful about how you use your sexual energy, as we are still in the healing process from past relationships. It might not be wise to fall quickly into a sexual relationship with someone or the ex you just broke up with.

In chapter five, we will discuss how to approach re-entering the dating world. For now, consider channeling your sexual energy into creative projects, such as dancing, writing, exercising, cooking, or something else that you've always wanted to do. In my experience, and the experience of the women I work with, men LOVE hearing about the jade egg. They find it a major turn-on and become curious about you. As you are increasing your sexual energy, just be mindful about how you wield your power, ok, goddess? (If you are in need of a jade egg, please visit my site where you can purchase one: letgoletgoddess.com.)

Sacred Self Assignment #4
Jade Egg and Yoni Ritual

A Special Note: I have created a ritual of initiation into the sexual arts of the jade egg. So whether you are an egg veteran or newcomer, you will gain many benefits from this ritual. It's designed to be used with a new egg, but you can use it also to rededicate an egg you already have.

Tools: Jade egg, sea salt, pink candles, pink flowers, half gallon milk, paper and pen, handheld mirror, sweet-smelling oils or perfume (rose, sandalwood, or orange oil are recommended)

Preparation: You will need to cleanse your jade egg prior to this. Boil water and pour over the egg. Do not boil the egg. Add sea salt to energetically cleanse it. Let egg sit inside boiled water and salt for a minimum of 30 minutes. (You can clean your egg this way from time to time, but you do not need to do this after every use. Clean egg with a natural soap in between use.) Afterward, you can smudge with incense, such as sage. You can also energetically charge your egg by leaving it to soak up sun or moonlight.

Part 1: Sweet Goddess Bath

Ritual

We will begin with a bath to cleanse our auric field.

1. Gather your pink candles. (Pink is the color of sexual energy in the Taoist tradition.)

2. Gather your pink flowers.

3. Run a nice, warm bath. Pour in the milk, while saying a prayer asking that it nourish and cleanse you. Milk is also symbolic of fertility and abundance. I especially like to use goat's milk.

4. Sprinkle some petals from the flowers into your bath water. Leave some flowers in a vase to beautify your home or altar.

5. Add some drops of perfume or essential oil, such as sandalwood, orange, or rose oil. If you have a rose quartz crystal or egg, you can put it inside your bath to energize it further.

6. Spend at least 30 minutes luxuriating in your bath. Think sweet, loving thoughts about yourself. Recite affirmations, while placing your left hand on your heart and right hand on your yoni.

Self-Love Affirmations

1. I am filled with love for myself, and this beautiful love shines to all I encounter.

2. I bow to the goddess in me and all who encounter me also bow to her. I honor the spirit of the Divine in everyone I meet.

3. My yoni is the sacred abode of the Goddess—I feed her pure love and light. She is the seat of my creativity; I have the power to birth whatever I desire.

Part 2: Yoni Gazing and Love Letter

1. Once you leave the bath, lovingly oil yourself.

2. Naked, lie down on your bed. Take a handheld mirror or even use the reverse camera on your phone. Take some time to look at your yoni. Many of us never take time to gaze at our goddess, unless we are seeing if something is "wrong." Look at your yoni with soft loving eyes. If we want others to look at our yonis with love and respect, we must as well.

3. Once you finish your yoni gazing, take some paper and begin writing a love letter to her. Imagine that you are your own lover. How would you want someone to talk to your yoni? What would your ideal lover say to her? How would they honor you and your sacred space? If you can radiate this within, you will attract this.

4. Once you finish, read the letter out loud. Feel the warm energy of self-love radiate throughout your body.

Part 3: Jade-Egg Ritual

1. Take your jade egg into your hands. Just take a moment, breathe deeply, and feel the energy of the stone. Jade is a crystal, and crystals carry energy. We can program crystals with our intention to help activate their energy. Take some time to meditate with your stone in your hand. Speak whatever intention you desire to the stone.

2. Lie naked on your back. Rest the jade egg on your belly or somewhere nearby. Rub your hands together and give yourself a massage to your breasts, womb,

ovaries, and yoni. Touch yourself in circular motions with gentle, loving hands.

3. Once you finish the massage, take the jade egg and place it in your left hand and place it over your heart. Place your right hand over your yoni. Breathe in and out sending loving energy from your heart to your yoni.

4. When you feel you are ready, place the jade egg at the entrance to your yoni. Ask your yoni for permission to begin this practice. Place the tip of the jade egg into your yoni and breathe in. As you breathe in, squeeze the jade egg with your yoni, and as you breathe out, relax and allow your yoni to open. Apply pressure to the egg and gently guide it in, continuing the breathing pattern until the jade egg is securely inside. Imagine your yoni drinking in the egg.

5. Once the egg is in, you can practice by inhaling and squeezing the egg with your yoni (contract your muscles as if you're trying to hold your urine in) and breathing out and relaxing. As you do this, the egg is moving up and down your yoni massaging the various reflexology zones that lie there.

6. You can also imagine your yoni canal divided into three parts (lower, middle, and upper) and practice isolating each part by squeezing each section separately in sets of nine. Some sections might be easier to isolate than others.

7. Enjoy this practice by having an attitude of play with it. You can leave the egg in for about 15 minutes, if you are just beginning your journey with the egg, and then gradually keep it in for longer periods of time. The egg is safe to sleep with inside you and might bring you sweet dreams.

8. You might end your practice however you like. Feel free to self-pleasure, as your energy might be extremely aroused.

~~~~~

Congratulations! You have become an initiate into some of the sacred teachings of the Goddess! These practices, though fairly simple, when done consistently can transform your spirit, body, and mind. Many years ago, ancient cultures would take their young women away once they reached puberty and train them on what it meant to be a woman in that particular society. The same thing would happen with young men.

They were not left in the dark to grapple with the meaning of womanhood, as there was a community of wise elders to ensure the young would learn what was needed to grow into an adult. Unfortunately, like many of the ancient ways, rites of passage are foreign to people in Western cultures, and many of us fall into a crisis when we try to figure out for ourselves what being a woman means.

Savor these ancient rites I share with you. As you honor your body-temple on a regular basis, you will notice how both your inner world and outer world transforms. When you recognize the goddess within you, others will as well. As Rumi said,

"The sky will bow to your beauty, if you do."

This bow is not one of an ego-driven thirst for recognition, but one that embodies the meaning of the anjali mudra in yoga. A mudra is a symbolic gesture. To perform anjali mudra, place your palms together over the center of your heart, lower your head, and say, "Namaste," which translates to, "the Divine in me, bows to the Divine in you."

Goddesses, I bow to you! Allow the world around you to swoon and throw kisses at your feet as you shine in your inner radiance. Worship all of you: breasts, yoni, legs, earlobes, eyelashes, ankles, mind, heart, and soul.

In the words of Ntozake Shange,

"i found God in myself and I loved her/ i loved her fiercely."

Chapter 4
Keep It Moving!

"On and on and on and on.
My cipher keeps moving like a rolling stone."

—Erykah Badu

You might have hated me in high school. I was all over the place—captain of the debate team, assistant editor of the yearbook, honor roll student, practically every writing contest I entered I won—and if you drove down Broad Street in Philadelphia, you'd see my face blasted 80-feet high on a wall. I was the overachiever, goodie-goodie girl. While many of my friends were having their first kisses, I was studying the government's current policy on juvenile delinquency.

I watched my older sibling struggle to gain the freedom to just be "one of the boys," while I easily etched out my independence. I built an extracurricular life for myself, always staying late after school to rehearse a show, help a teacher, or take theater classes.

Sadly, while I made progress, I watched many of my family and community members get consumed by the streets. Teenage pregnancies, drugs, and crime were common. Many of them were just as brilliant and capable as me, if not more so, but we were separated by one major thing, inertia.

Inertia is defined as, "a tendency to do nothing or remain unchanged." My mind and my body were always actively discovering, exploring, and questioning. This kept me moving into new levels of knowledge and experiences. Many of the young people I saw were stuck—stuck in patterns of harmful thinking in an environment where, far too often, very little was expected of them. So, with too much time on their hands without constructive activities that expanded their mind, they fell to the vices of the concrete jungle.

When we become stagnant, we become susceptible to dubious behaviors and negative influences. Now that we have done lots of internal healing work, we're going to focus on keeping our lives full of positive activities to channel our energy into.

When people fall back in with an ex, even if it's just for sex, it is often because they're bored and scared to be alone. They fall back into what is "comfortable" and remain stuck in the inertia of an unfulfilling relationship. There are also people who do not go back to their ex, but become depressed because their life feels empty and meaningless without a partner to share it with.

However, we are powerful goddesses who know that there is so much more waiting for us to discover! We are going to keep it moving! Now, the movement I speak of is not mere "busyness" for busyness' sake. We are not trying to stay occupied to distract ourselves from our problems as some people do. No, we are doing the internal work needed to create inner peace in our lives so when we move, it is not from a place of lack, but from a place of flow.

We are flowing in a current of positive energy that brings us into alignment with new and exciting opportunities, events, knowledge, and people. The simple fact that you are reading this book shows that you are in the flow of the universe. As Erykah Badu says,

"I go on and on and on and on.
My cipher keeps moving like a rolling stone."

What is a cipher? If you have ever watched rappers freestyle, you know that they stand in a circle that they call a cipher, and each person goes around the circle and drops some lyrics. A cipher is a circle of energy that keeps going and going. There is no end and no beginning to a circle. This is the energy flow of life. We keep moving, we keep flowing, and each time we discover something new and deepen our learning.

In this chapter we are going to focus on how to keep our energy moving, so that we do not fall into inertia or boredom and backtrack into the patterns and behaviors we have worked to heal and overcome.

Sacred Sadhana

It was 5 a.m.—my eyes spied on my cellphone— although by the heavy drape of darkness, it could have been midnight. From the sounds pouring into my ears, I wasn't the only one up. Life was buzzing all over the mountains. The song of the coquí frog seemed to be continuing from last night. After a quick shower, I began my trek up the hill to the yoga studio. The other sisters and I walked in silence, as was our mandate, our flashlights like fireflies dancing in the twilight.

The ground was squishy from yesterday's rain, and twice I almost slid on the muddy rocks. Once a day, the skies of Utuado, Puerto Rico, seemed to open the floodgates they could no longer hold back, bathing the earth in their lush rains like an orgasm. Standing in the open-air yoga studio deck, I went through my asana practice, as dawn spread its orange fingers across the horizon. I let go of several layers of clothes, as my body started to heat.

Facing the mountain, I found a deep reservoir of strength. A mist caressed the early morning as I went through yoga postures, qi gong, breath work, and meditation, followed by a sweet half-conscious Shavasana pose. Every movement was a prayer and a dance—a dedication to my body and the practice of entering into the temple of myself. As I laid, back flat, sinking into the ground, everything around me dissipated. Suddenly there was no yoga, no mountains, no creatures, no sounds, nothing. Even my mind existed no more. I just was . . .

I was blessed enough to complete my yoga teacher training in the lush mountains of Puerto Rico. Every day we were up at 5 a.m. to begin our 90-minute sadhana practice. This practice was to include yoga poses, meditation, and resting in corpse pose or Shavasana. But it could also include prayer, walking in nature, dancing, and even singing.

Sadhana simply means daily spiritual practice. Prior to my training, I did have some form of practice that was mostly inconsistent. Yoga was mostly done inside a formal class, and I'd start off the year motivated, but as time went on, I became too lazy to get up and meditate or pray.

But having the experience of being tucked away near the mountains, away from technology, and being made to practice daily for 90 minutes at sunrise, I was transformed. For me now, my sadhana is a necessity, like sleep or water. I must take time every day to get plugged into my Source. Here is a quote about sadhana:

"What is sadhana?
It's a committed prayer.
It is something which you want to do,
have to do, and which is being done by you. . . .
Sadhana is self-enrichment. It is not something,
which is done to please somebody or to gain something.
Sadhana is a personal process in which
you bring out your best."

—Yogi Bhajan

So, having a daily spiritual practice isn't something you do to avoid punishment or to fulfill an obligation. Many of us were raised to fulfill certain duties that made us a part of whatever religion our parents claimed. Many of these things were done begrudgingly, in order to avoid chastisement or simply because we were told to.

Sadhana is not that. Sadhana is you tapping into *you* for *you*. I invite you to create a daily spiritual practice for yourself—if you don't have one already. Our spiritual practices can be just as unique as we are, but I will focus on three components: prayer, meditation, and movement. The purpose of these three activities is to raise our frequency and become aligned with our higher self.

As we travel throughout our day-to-day life, we often carry stress from our workplace, families, finances, etc. According to the American Psychological Association, more than 77 percent of people have physical symptoms because of stress, such as headaches, backaches, and high blood pressure. More than 73 percent of people have psychological symptoms as a result of stress, such as anxiety, worry, and depression.

In fact, women are more likely than men to report having physical and emotional symptoms of stress. While we can't always control what happens around us, we can control how we respond. While we have done this marvelous internal work to release past patterns and baggage from old relationships and tap into our bliss, we are still going to have triggers that bring a stressful response in our bodies.

Having a daily sadhana practice is a great way to regulate yourself as you move through life. It's like the water hole the elephant stops at to cool and hydrate itself. Imagine, what if the animals in the Sahara just kept trekking across the blazing desert without pausing to rest? They would break down and eventually die.

Many of us feel broken down or "dehydrated," because we are not consistently partaking in the water of spirit. As we are shifting our vibration to attract the love we truly deserve and desire, we must first become full spiritually. So, when we meet our future life partner, we are not looking for someone else to complete us, we are a whole, looking for another whole to create a spiral of infinite love.

A Time for Everything

The first thing you need to do is set a consistent time for your sadhana. Granted, spiritual communion can happen anytime, sometimes the most spectacular experiences can be spontaneous. But by developing a regular routine, you help to avoid spiritual burnout. Many of us wait until we are in crisis to use our spiritual tools, but in truth, one should always be in communion with the Divine. This helps us to navigate the bumps along the way much easier.

Many people find that having a morning practice gets them ready for their day and casts a stream of positive energy forward to what lies ahead. I highly suggest having a consistent morning practice. As a single mother, it is important for me to wake up prior to my son and enjoy time by myself.

There is something about the quiet that exists in the wee hours of the morning, not just in my house but also on the earth. Outside the energy is still and calm, making my spiritual communion much easier. The time period when we are between morning and night is special. It represents the space between the subconscious and conscious states of being.

This is the state where it is easiest to reprogram the mind and spirit with ideas and behaviors. We are the most receptive when the earth, like us, is awakening to a new day.

This balance of lunar and solar, or male and female energies, is perfect for activities such as prayer, meditation, and yoga.

Another ideal time for sadhana is just before bed. As we are ending the day and on our way to slipping into the subconscious realm, we can seal our night with spiritual practices. Our conscious behavior is controlled by our subconscious mind, and when we do our work at night, we can create powerful shifts in our subconscious. I like to do more elaborate rituals at night, during the new or full moon or other significant times.

A nighttime meditation or yoga routine could be a perfect way to unwind after a long, hard day. Find what time works best for you to have a daily practice. The most important thing is consistency. After getting up daily at 5 a.m. during my yoga teacher training, doing my practice in the morning has become routine for me. Most of the time, my sadhana is like a lover, whose open arms I love to revel in.

When I'm flowing in my practice, it is almost as if time stands still. There were days when I became so indulgent and spent so much time doing yoga and meditation that I only had 20 minutes to rush and get dressed for work. I would go to work almost or outright late, not because I overslept, but because I was doing yoga! I would feel so good that it was hard to pull away. (However, I am not recommending you show up late to work and tell your boss you got caught up doing yoga.)

Then there are days, of course, when I am tired and my body feels tight, and I want no parts of yoga or meditation. But I do not allow myself to stay there. If I miss a day, I make sure to get right back on track. My amazing yoga teacher even told us, yes, sometimes sadhana is lusciously sleeping in some mornings—we must listen to what our body needs overall, but if we want to maintain balance, we must make our sadhana a consistent practice. Though our sadhana practice can contain anything, we will focus on three things: prayer, meditation, and movement.

Prayer

"For me, prayer is a surge of the heart;
it is a simple look turned toward heaven,
it is a cry of recognition and of love,
embracing both trial and joy."

St. Thérèse de Lisieux

"Prayer is the soul's sincere desire.
Your desire is your prayer.
It comes out of your deepest needs and
it reveals the things you want in life."

Joseph Murphy

When many of us think of prayer, we envision someone kneeling in a gothic-looking church with stained-glass windows, asking for mercy or forgiveness. Or maybe as a child, we imagined God to be a big "Santa Claus in the sky," who we could pray to, to get what we wanted. Whatever your vision or introduction to prayer was, I ask that you expand your idea of prayer.

I believe of all spiritual technology, prayer is probably the most ancient and intimate. Many of us pray all day, but do so unaware. Our thoughts are prayers. Our hopes and desires are prayers. We must begin to become conscious about our prayers and pray with purpose!

Prayer to me is simply invoking Source Energy, by whatever name or names you call it, into an intimate conversation with you. It is an emotional beckoning to invite spirit to intercede for us on the invisible realm in ways that we cannot do in the physical. Sometimes, the asking might be only for the strength to do what we know we need to do. At other times, we pray to summon miracles. Eckhart Tolle said,

*"If the only prayer we ever said was thank you
that would be enough."*

Prayers of gratitude are powerful and magnificent, because whatever we focus on expands. When you give thanks, you are saying, "Yes, more of this please!" and the universe reflects that back to you.

Many of us spend too much time worrying, which is really praying for what we do not want. Worrying is the unconscious directing of our thoughts toward that which we do not desire. We must mind our thoughts, which will make our prayers even more effective. If you're praying for abundance, but your thoughts reflect lack, you are going to receive lack. Our thoughts reflect our dominant vibrational patterns. Shift your thoughts and speak your desires through prayer.

Prayer can be both the call and the answer. Often, as I am praying, I realize it is more a talk to uplift my spirit. I am in fact not even asking the Divine to do anything. I am invoking the Divine from within by the power and conviction of my words, which causes a natural shift in my energy, and naturally I fall into alignment to receive what it is I want. This is called affirmative prayer. It is not a weak pleading prayer out of fear. It is praying with complete faith that you already have what you are asking for!

When we pray, it should not be from a place of begging or desperation. It can, however, be from a place of surrender. Surrender is beautiful. Surrender means we have released control and ask for the highest good to manifest in our lives.

Prayer should also be from a place of faith, expecting to receive what you are asking for or something far greater. When you finish praying, you should feel lighter, brighter, and stronger. You should be filled with conviction. The most important aspects of prayer are faith and humility. Ask, receive, believe, and give the utmost thanks!

Meditation

If prayer is talking to God, meditation could be considered God, or our higher self, talking back to us. While prayer may invoke the Divine seemingly from without, meditation invokes the Divine from within. For me, a full spiritual practice contains both. I often begin my day in solitude and prayer and slide easily into the quietude of meditation.

Often the answers we are seeking are already within us, if we could just quiet our mental chatter and become still, we can enter into a sacred dialogue with our higher self. Have you ever been in a "conversation" with someone who just keeps talking and talking and never allows you to get a word in? Well, that is what many of us do to the Divine. We unload but we do not receive. That kind of practice will yield slow results spiritually.

"Meditation is the dissolution of thoughts in eternal awareness or pure consciousness without objectification, knowing without thinking, merging finitude in infinity."

—Swami Sivananda

I am an overthinker. For many years, I have often prided myself on how "smart" I thought I was. Until life really hit. Heartbreak. Divorce. Confusion. Then I realized no matter how "smart" I thought I was, it was not my brain that would bring me peace or clear solutions.

I had to actually learn to "un-think" and quiet what the Buddha referrers to as "the monkey mind." The Buddhists use the metaphor of a monkey swinging from vine to vine in the jungle to reflect what we do with our thoughts. We jump from thought to thought, unfocused and undisciplined, swinging wildly through the wilderness of our heads, often making ourselves bananas!

A major benefit of meditation is to bring order to our chaotic mind. When our minds are clear, we feel calm and relaxed. The solutions to many of our problems arrive effortlessly. In really deep meditative states, we get to touch the face of the Divine, feel our oneness with all, and merge into the sea of the infinite. We feel the truth of who we are and that as Abraham Hicks says,

"You can be, do or have anything you want!"

Have you ever been extremely stressed and tried to make a decision? You usually can't, right? When you do, it is usually a rash decision you wind up regretting later. Life has taught me the importance of slowing down and focusing on my breath.

I have left my cellphone on the street corner outside Trader Joes because I was stressed. I have left the keys to my house in the door, closed it behind me, and later spent an hour looking for them because I was rushing. Meditation teaches us to slow down, breathe correctly—deeply and slowly from the diaphragm. Whenever I begin a coaching call, I always start with a short breathing exercise so that I and the client can center ourselves. This puts us both in a heightened state of receptivity so an effective session can happen.

Meditation unlocks the gate to the subconscious. While we use the conscious mind mostly in our day-to-day activities—cooking, cleaning, working, etc.—our actions are actually controlled by our subconscious. The subconscious is a million times more powerful then the conscious mind. Brain scientists estimate that 95–99 percent of how we operate in our lives is from subconscious programming. When we try to make changes in ourselves from our conscious mind, most of the time it simply doesn't stick.

This is why the majority of people fail with their New Year's resolutions. It's not because they are lazy, it is because they haven't tapped into their subconscious to give power to their goals. Imagine an iceberg—the conscious mind is the tip jutting out of the water that you see, the subconscious is the majority of the iceberg hidden underwater that sinks ships! The "ship" many of us sink are our lives, because we are ignoring an important aspect of our being.

How do we tap into the subconscious? That's right, through meditation. This is why I asked you to meditate so much in the beginning chapters, as we were asking for clarity about our past relationships and working on letting go of negative patterns. If we want to change our behavior, or get clear on something, plugging into the subconscious through meditation is the way to go. As we slow down our breath, we change our brain waves from active to slower frequencies. These slower frequencies are linked to the subconscious and hold the key to unlocking the power of our being.

There are several brainwave states identified by scientists. The **beta state** is linked to our normal, waking consciousness. For many adults, this is the dominant state from which we access logic and reasoning, highly coveted skills in Western society.

I also liken this state to a masculine way of being. As modern women, we often can spend too much time in this state, which can leave us feeling tense and cold. Being in this state for too long can lead to anxiety and restlessness. It's no wonder that the majority of people in this modern society experience stress and stress-related ailments so often. Our society values action. We are taught to speed up instead of slow down and to use our "brain" to fix problems. While we do need access to the beta state, we will be unbalanced and unhealthy if we remain fixed there.

The next state is the **alpha state.** This is the state of deep relaxation we experience during meditation. It heightens our ability to visualize, learn, and have deep concentration. It is the gateway to the subconscious and lies at the base of our conscious mind. It is the voice of our intuition.

The third state is **theta**. This is the deep meditation and light sleeping state. When we experience rapid eye movement (REM) sleep where dreaming happens, we have entered this state, the realm of the subconscious. Theta is said to house a deep connection to spirit and is experienced most often while we are drifting off to sleep from alpha and going into delta, the next state after theta. Our deep patterns and programs exist in the theta brainwave, and it's also where we have access to vivid insights, visualizations, and creativity. I imagine that many of the prophets, seers, and shamans experience this state quite frequently.

Delta is the slowest frequency and is experienced in deep, dreamless sleep and deep meditation where consciousness is detached. This is considered the gateway to the unconscious, where we have access to the realm of the universal mind. This frequency is connected to deep healing and regeneration. This is why it's important to get enough sleep, so you experience those delta waves and your body has the opportunity to heal itself.

So in our work with meditation, we are tapping into the alpha and theta brainwaves (and maybe even delta) to access our deep subconscious. Adding meditation to your daily practice will allow you to make quantum leaps in your personal and spiritual development. As we slow down from being externally focused, we find a temple deep within ourselves wherein lies peace, wisdom, love, and luminosity.

Movement

"Movement is a medicine for creating change in a person's physical, emotional, and mental states."

—Carol Welch

A little earlier, I wrote about my experience in Puerto Rico of doing 5 a.m. sadhanas every day. If you had told me several years ago that I'd be training to be a yoga teacher, I'd have looked at you like you were crazy. I practiced yoga on and off for years but never consistently. As a drama major in college, at a physically based acting studio, I was used to doing some kind of movement on a fairly regular basis but had no real practice of my own. I was never very athletic, haven't been in dance class since I was two, nor did I consider myself particularly flexible. I wasn't the "typical" image of a female yoga teacher—a short, blond-haired girl from Vermont named Amy, who's an ex-ballerina.

I'm more on the tall side, "big boned" with thick thighs, a chocolate girl, whose mother named her Tameka. But in finding my body through daily movement, I found myself. We hold tension in our bodies that needs to be released through regular exercises. Yoga for me is a prayer. If I go a few days without it, not only does my body feel tight, but my spirit feels ill at ease. I will break into a yoga pose with some deep breathing when I feel sad or anxious.

Scientists have discovered that our brains become wired in certain ways based on our past experiences. Many times when a problem arises, we are not really reacting to that current situation, we simply default to how our minds and bodies have become conditioned to respond to stress.

Let's say your boss yells at you and you get so furious that all you can do is cry hot, angry tears. The crying response is possibly one that got programmed into you when an authority figure, such as a parent, yelled at you as a child. We must work to undo this programming and create different neural pathways in our brain, so we can have the response we really want to have, like we did through our "Re-Patterning" Meditation in chapter two.

As our mind becomes conditioned to certain behaviors, so does the body become conditioned by painful memories to hold in tension and pain in certain areas. When we exercise, we give the body permission to release these tensions and also build strength and flexibility.

There are many types of movement we can do with our bodies. I encourage you to explore and find your own favorites that suit your personality and your physical, spiritual, and emotional needs. I am going to highlight a few of my favorites to practice. Try sampling a class, or buying a DVD to discover what works for you.

Yoga

Yoga literally means, "to yoke." We are joining or "yoking" ourselves to the Divine through a practice that aims to heal both the body and mind. Yoga began thousands of years ago in ancient India and is tremendously popular here in the Western world. The benefits of yoga are many, including the improved function of our digestive, hormonal, respiratory, and circulatory systems.

Yoga aids in the detoxification of our body and in the strengthening of our core. The focus on breathing in yoga brings deep relaxation. The asanas or poses help to take us out of our "monkey mind." To truly get into a pose you have to be focused. Postures become difficult to maintain if you're busy thinking about what you want to make for dinner or the bills that must get paid. This is why I personally love yoga. It forces you to be in the moment, which is one of the great goals of meditations.

Now there are many types of yoga: hatha, kundalini, vinyasa, ashtanga, bikram, etc. Some styles focus more on athleticism and challenging poses, others encourage a freer flow, some are more ritualistic and others are done in a heated room of 100 degrees. Some people try yoga once and find it too difficult, but I say don't give up! Sometimes, it takes finding the style or teacher that is right for you.

Take your time and find what works for your body. I highly encourage practicing yoga at least once a week for 90 minutes, or several shorter sessions three to four times a week. A complete practice will include meditation and ample time spent in Shavasana, a pose where you lie on your back on the floor. Interestingly enough, this pose, though simple, can also be the most challenging, as it requires you to surrender.

As you become more comfortable you'll be able to choreograph your own yoga routines. In the words of yogi Amit Ray,

"Exercises are like prose, whereas yoga is the poetry of movements. Once you understand the grammar of yoga; you can write your poetry of movements."

The deeply spiritual side of yoga is also centered on raising our primal energy, kundalini, which lies at the base of the spine to meet our god consciousness, which lies in our head or crown.

Kundalini is also known as the goddess Shakti, the dynamic energy that empowers the universe. It is believed that as the kundalini travels through our spine, it purifies various spiritual centers, thus freeing us from our ego and releasing our spiritual gifts. Through the practice of yoga, many people reach nirvana or enlightenment as the energy flows unobstructed through their bodies. Yoga makes me feel sexy and blissful. It is my key to letting go of tension and feeling an orgasmic release through movement.

Qi Gong

Qi gong is an ancient Chinese practice that involves physical poses, breath work, and focused intention. Similar to yoga, it moves energy through subtle channels for the benefit of the mind, spirit, and body. It is the combination of two words, *qi,* meaning life force energy, and *gong,* meaning a skill that is cultivated through practice.

There are many different types of qi gong, some increase the amount of qi for better health and energy, while some circulate and use the qi to cleanse the body, still others store the qi for later use or healing. The qi flows through various energy meridians in the body and connects to the elements of earth, fire, water, metal, and wood.

Qi gong is not as popular or as commercialized as yoga. It is not as "sexy," meaning you are not made to do head stands or sweat in a sauna wearing booty shorts, but it is highly effective. Qi gong is the foundation for many martial arts—as it gives practitioners a keen sense of focus and attunement with the energy of their own bodies.

Being able to harness and direct your qi awakens your inner powers and natural healing ability. When doing qi gong, you tend to repeat the movement in a rhythmic pattern and focus on a color, sound, or energy system in your body. The practice of qi gong has been noted to improve the lymphatic, digestive, respiratory, and circulatory functions of the body. Many practitioners also note an increase in their vitality levels.

I often include qi gong after my yoga practice. While yoga makes me feel like a goddess, qi gong makes me feel like superwoman! I use the yoga to open my body and get my energy flowing and qi gong to direct it even more specifically through the various meridians of my body. While practicing qi gong, I will often go into a trance-like state and the feeling of qi flowing through me is palpable. It is amazing to me how movements that are so simple are so powerful.

Many people are attracted to qi gong because of the ease of the movements—there is much less room for injury than in yoga, and anybody of any age or body type can practice. Qi gong can also have a healing effect on the emotions, as certain sounds are used during the movements to vent toxic energy trapped in our organs, where Taoists believe our emotions are housed. If these emotions are not released safely, the trapped energy can lead to disease. A regular qi gong practice allows us to "air out" so we can be more balanced and whole. I will often do the healing sounds of qi gong when upset. It is a good way for me to acknowledge what I am feeling and release it.

Now, finding a qi gong class is not as easy as finding a yoga class, but doing a search in your city is worth a try. There are also videos you can find. I teach various qi gong exercises in my online classes, workshops, and goddess retreats.

If you go to my website, you will find information on my current workshops, retreats, and classes where qi gong is offered. Sign-up for it at letgoletgoddess.com

Dance

"Shake ya ass! Watch yourself! Shake ya ass!
Show me whatcha workin' wit!"

—Mystikal

I love to shake my ass! Don't you? When we dance, the body releases endorphins that gives us a natural high. Dancing releases stress and reduces depression. High-energy dancing will also increase your heart rate, burn calories, lower your blood pressure, improve your muscle tone, give you increased energy, and most of all make you feel good!

There are many different types of dance. You can take a class on belly dance, hip-hop, kizomba, pole dance, West African, samba, salsa, flamenco, or even ballroom dancing. Whatever type of dance floats your boat, go do it! I am also a proponent of turning on some music and having my own dance party. I believe we should dance every single day. It gives us an excuse to be happy and to sweat. I often include dance in my sadhana practice and sometimes my sadhana is just dance. No yoga, no qi gong, not even a meditation, just DANCE!

I must confess, while I am a qi-gong-namaste-green-juice-drinking holistic yogi, I feel like I missed my calling as a stripper or a dancehall girl! My favorite kind of dance is sensual, seductive, and mostly nude. I love, love dancing to reggae, wining my waist and twerking my butt. Yes, twerking (or trying to anyway). These kinds of dance movements are widely demonized and misunderstood. Many people are afraid to see women connect to their sexual power. Now, of course there are occasions when this dance is used to objectify women as props for the male gaze, but there is something so much deeper at work that needs to be recognized.

So called "twerking" has many links to dances of the African diaspora, especially the Mapouka from the Ivory Coast in West Africa. If you have ever taken an African or Afro-Caribbean dance class, you can testify that—

Number one: it's an INTENSE, amazing workout, and

Number two: that a lot of the moves focus on isolations of the hips, pelvis, and buttocks.

These movements build strength and control of the pelvic floor and core muscles, which are important when it comes to childbirth and overall health.

On another level, these dances help to circulate qi in our lower tantien, or energy center. In Taoism, our lower tantien, located three finger widths below our navel is where our life force and sexual energy is stored and generated. The lower tantien is a major point of focus in martial arts and is considered to be our "root."

When it is strong, we have increased energy to support our physical and spiritual bodies. Tantrically speaking, these dances circulate energy through our first and second chakras, which are connected to our feelings of safety and creativity, respectively. When these chakras are balanced, we have a greater connection to our sensuality and abundance.

Belly dancing is another form of dance that is great for women's health and spirituality, as the dance reflects movements natural to women's bodies. The isolations performed in these dances bring strength and healing to the reproductive system and are believed to have originally been used to assist women in childbirth. When energy is flowing properly in this area, stagnant qi is dispersed, which helps to prevent or alleviate feminine reproductive issues, such as painful menses and fibroids.

I believe all women should do dances that involve isolating and rotating their hips and pelvis, like the Jamaican "wine" every day. Dances such as the wine and twerk are often done without consciousness, but when we add the level of awareness that not only are we having fun, but we are also healing ourselves, we can revolutionize our health and sexuality. I'll give you a tip, do these dances while wearing your yoni egg! Oh, goddess, that is yummy!

Open to Bliss Schedule

So we just have explored the importance of having a sadhana or daily practice that includes prayer, meditation, yoga, qi gong, dancing, and twerking. There are so many others things we could add to the list, but this is a great start. As you explore these exercises, you will encounter other things that will help you get in alignment with your higher self.

As we focus on keeping it moving, so we don't backtrack into negative patterns or unhealthy relationships, I invite you to create an Open to Bliss Schedule. This schedule will allow you to fill your time with meaningful and luscious activities that will keep you focused and fulfilled.

Open to Bliss Process

Make a list of 10–15 things you love to do. This could be anything from biking to napping to going to concerts or eating chocolate.

Create a schedule for the next two weeks in which you do each of those things at least once.

Include a proposed plan for your daily sadhana. Be sure to include prayer, meditation, and some form of movement. Also include your yoni egg, breast massage, etc., in your sadhana or as a bliss practice.

Plan on taking a dance or yoga class once a week, if time and money allows. Be sure to include space for relaxation and pure pleasure!

Here's an example of my Open to Bliss Schedule:

Sunday	Monday	Tuesday	Wednesday	Thursday	Friday	Saturday
Sadhana Morning meditation Prayer to my ancestors	Sadhana Meditation Yoga Qi gong with yoni egg	Sadhana Meditation Yoga Qi gong Long breast massage	Sadhana Sleep in	Sadhana Meditation Yoga Qi gong	Sadhana DANCE!	Sadhana Morning mediation
Bliss Practice Hot yoga class	Bliss Practice Long yoni egg practice	Bliss Practice Netflix night	Bliss Practice Bellydance class	Bliss Practice Sweet treat (ice cream)	Bliss Practice Take a goddess bath.	Bliss Practice Go to the spa. Have Ethiopian food for dinner.

Goddess Sister Circle

When going through a breakup or when living the single life, no matter what, you will have bouts of loneliness. It is important to have a circle of people to support you, give you a shoulder to cry on, and help you to laugh through the tears. You also need people you can have fun with and paint the town red when you feel like it.

I cannot even express how important my sister circle has been to me. I have been blessed with relationships with other women who help me maintain my sanity and let loose. We all need someone to talk to, laugh, and be outraged with. My friends and I even have a group text message that allows us to share the highs and lows we experience throughout the day.

I am not a "homebody," so I enjoy going out to dinner on a Friday or Saturday night or an occasional party with my girlfriends. It gives me something to look forward to. Once a month or so, my sisters and I all go to the spa together and spend the entire day. I very much look forward to this day. I get to indulge in relaxation and pure pleasure with good company. On this day, there is no agenda other than to luxuriate. I encourage you to budget for a day like this once a month for yourself. Clear the calendar, get a babysitter, and just focus on you!

Now, I often hear some women complain about how you can't trust other women and how they don't have female friends. Some of them tell stories of how they were betrayed or stabbed in the back by their best friends. While these feelings might be valid and betrayal is never easy to experience, once again I ask you to look in the mirror. If you are one of those women who constantly have issues with other women, and have trouble forming positive female relationships, I encourage you to go back and do the "Mirror, Mirror" exercise—this time focused on female friendships. If there is a definite pattern of difficulty creating bonds with other women, then you must find the root of that pattern and heal it. Women need other women—period.

As you keep it moving, you will truly get caught up in the love affair of your own life. We all need things to look forward to and an inner motivation that keeps us growing. Try exploring new things, foods, and places. Go rock climbing, paintballing, start writing your own novel, learn to sew, take a Thai food cooking class, or book a photo shoot for yourself. There is a buffet of experiences waiting for you to savor!

While on this journey, I took a trip to Jamaica, all by my pretty brown self. The sheer joy I got from not having to negotiate with anyone but me was so liberating. The blue of the ocean, the majesty of the mountains, and the coolness of the springs were all just for me to touch and taste. I didn't have to check in with anyone else to see what they wanted to do, I did whatever the hell *I* wanted! It was such a healing experience.

We need to be so happy with ourselves that we feel comfortable enough to luxuriate in our own company. We are never truly alone, when we are one with ourselves, for then we are one with creation.

In the words of Osho,

"Take hold of your own life.
See that the whole existence is celebrating.
These trees are not serious, these birds are not serious.
The rivers and the oceans are wild,
and everywhere there is fun,
everywhere there is joy and delight.
Watch existence,
listen to the existence and become part of it."

Items Needed for Chapter 5 Open to the New

- ✓ Yellow flowers
- ✓ ½ gallon cow's milk
- ✓ 1 quart goat's milk
- ✓ Cinnamon
- ✓ Brown sugar
- ✓ Honey
- ✓ 1 small bottle of Florida water (find in grocery store, botanica, or online)
- ✓ 1 bottle of white wine
- ✓ Sandalwood oil or sweet perfume
- ✓ Sandalwood incense
- ✓ Seven-day yellow candle
- ✓ Pumpkin
- ✓ Honey
- ✓ Five coins
- ✓ Knife
- ✓ Pen and paper

Chapter 5
Open to the New

"On a day
when the wind is perfect,
the sail just needs to open and
the world is full of beauty.
Today is such a day."

—Rumi

Goddess, you decided it was over, dug down deep and released the patterns from your past, committed to loving yourself, and you have filled your life with more bliss than you can stand, and now it is time to open to the new.

In the words of phenomenal woman Maya Angelou,

"Have enough courage to trust love one more time and always one more time."

Unless you've sworn off dating and being in a relationship again (which I know you haven't or won't feel that way for long), there will come a time when you'll want to step out and test the waters again. The person you are now is much different from the person you were in your last relationship. You've learned some lessons, experienced some powerful growth, and I'm sure you want a few different things this time than you did before. As a matter of fact, more than ever before, you are now surer of what you want in a relationship.

How do you know you're in fact "ready" to start dating again? How do you know that you've healed and are ready for a commitment? As Rumi says,

"On a day when the wind is perfect,
the sail just needs to open."

In other words, you will know. Trust your gut, and connect to your intuition. Find your "perfect wind." Don't feel a need to rush out there. I invite you to savor dating the same way you savored your healing practices.

I'm not going to give you a bunch of "rules" on dating, or tricks that will drive men wild. A woman in touch with her spirit, sensuality, and filled with the bliss of self-love is enough to drive any respectable man wild! So, if you want to know how and when to text a man back, you might want to research elsewhere. My basic stance on things like texting or calling is simply to treat other people the way you want to be treated. So, if you'd prefer someone to be responsive to texts, then you be responsive to texts. The mirror is always present! We attract what we are, so if you're playing games, trust me, you're going to attract someone who is playing games.

What I am going to discuss in this chapter is how to be open to receiving love—real love, the love you want, what I call your Most Compatible Soul Mate. This is the one who is ready and willing to help you achieve your greatest destiny and the most beautiful evolution of your spirit. Of course, I'm not saying you can't date and have fun. By all means, once you feel you're ready please do so, but always hold the vision of what you truly want.

As we begin dating again, we're going to have different experiences, some good, others bad, and certain ones are just plain ugly. I think it's important to have some context to the experiences you might have while dating, so I've made some "categories" for the various connections with men you might find as you are exploring and attracting your life partner.

The No Man

This man is just a NO. No connection, no attraction. Maybe you went out with him because you're bored, and he's a really nice guy. Maybe you want a free dinner—no judgment! (I've been there.) But you know that this is going nowhere. I advise you to enjoy the date, if you choose to entertain him, but do not lead him on. You wouldn't want anyone doing that to you, so even if he is fawning all over you, like every word that comes out your mouth is dipped in gold, don't abuse it. Take it for what it is, and keep it moving.

Hmmm . . . Not Quite Man

This is a man you might be attracted to. He looks good on the outside, has good qualities, a good job, etc., but he just doesn't ring your bells. You might go out for a few dates, but there is no "stickiness" factor between you. Your pheromones are not calling for him. You might be better off as friends. He's cool to hang out with, but clearly not the one for you.

Red Hot Man

This man comes to you and makes everything in your body scream. You are on fire, and you want him to put you out! The sexual attraction is at an all-time high, but the inner qualities that you really want are missing. You know that in the long term, he just won't do. Maybe he's emotionally unavailable, already in a relationship, juggling multiple women, or just not ready to settle down.

I'm not going to tell you not to enjoy an experience with Mr. Red Hot Man, but be honest about what you can handle. If you really want commitment, and this man is all about having fun, it might not be wise to keep hooking up with him. He might have just come into your life to throw some gasoline on your fire—allow that to be it. Don't keep going back thinking that your yoni magic is going to be so good that he's going to commit to you. You're going to wind up getting your feelings hurt. Enjoy him (or not) and let him go.

Soul Tie Man

This is a man who comes into your life to teach you a lesson. At the beginning you may confuse him with your Most Compatible Soul Mate. There is a strong connection and mutual attraction. You might have a lot in common. He might have some of the qualities you are looking for in your life partner, but as the relationship progresses, you realize he is not the one. He is most likely unavailable or has some other fatal flaw, and the relationship might be an emotional rollercoaster. You go through the ups and downs of trying to get him to give you what he simply cannot. Recognize this and allow yourself to move on.

The Soul Tie Man comes to get you ready for your true soul mate. He will mirror back to you your fears, some of what you want in a man and some of what you absolutely do not. This relationship can be painful to let go of, but once you realize he is taking the space of the one who is truly meant for you, you can allow yourself to move on.

Most Compatible Soul Mate

This is the one who comes ready to commit to you and evolve with you. He might not look like what you originally envisioned your life partner to look like, but he is just right. He is not perfect, but he is perfect for you. Your Most Compatible Soul Mate is someone who has incarnated with a complementary life purpose to you, and you two will come together to aid one another in the achievement of your destiny. You two can go much further together than you can alone, and love is the bonding force.

He comes as a balance to you and will in fact push your buttons, but it is a push to grow. He is invested in being a witness as you become your best self. He is not afraid to tell you the truth about yourself, because he believes in your highest good and wants the best for you. You support him and stand as his witness too. You are in love with his soul and committed to his evolution. This relationship is one of mutual love, expansion, and growth.

~~~~~

Please don't take these categories as hard-and-fast rules. Some men might in fact be a mixture of two categories. For example, I've seen women start dating Hmm . . . Not Quite Men and then become caught up in a Soul Tie-type relationship, as they allow the relationship to progress. I believe my ex-husband was a Hmm . . . Not Quite Man for me, but obviously we had a soul and karmic connection.

I only say that because I had Soul Tie relationships with men after my marriage, and those connections were actually much stronger than the one I had with my husband. I also don't mean to paint the Most Compatible Soul Mate relationship as perfect and pain free, it certainly is not. All relationships require work and all reflect the positive and negative within us. What differs in these types of soul mate relationships is the committed intention and ability to evolve together. This gives them the power to last.

I have had several Soul Tie relationships, and I've witnessed many of my friends and clients also have them. Often these relationships can be quite addicting, as the reflection of the other person of our light and dark can run really deep. I do believe that in *some* cases the Soul Tie can evolve into a lifelong Most Compatible Soul Mate. But often in those relationships, because they are so intense, there needs to be a break from each other, so that you can both evolve and grow.

You know the saying, "If you want something, let it go; if it is truly yours, it will come back to you." During the break, it is important for *both* parties to focus on their healing and evolution, so that when they come back together, it is with a stronger love and commitment to make the relationship work. If you are the only person doing the work or neither of you are doing the work, you will have the same issues you had before, and this time it will be worse. Both of you must commit to working on yourselves.

It is a different experience to get into a relationship from a place of love and desire for growth than from a place of deficit and looking for someone to complete you. It is my belief that when it comes time to enter into a relationship with your Most Compatible Soul Mate, there need not be any ultimatums, coercion, manipulation, or conniving to get this man to commit to you. He is available and ready to love you the way you deserved to be loved. Do not allow desperation to make you put pressure on a man to be with you. No matter how much you love this man, know your honor and your worth.

Also, if a man tells you he does not want a relationship, believe him! Don't think you're going to hang around and convince him to change his mind. If you allow yourself to continue to sleep with him, knowing your desires are not in alignment, just be ready to put on your big-girl panties when after months of "playing" girlfriend, he tells you he's seeing someone else or that he's still not ready for a commitment. The same thing applies to marriage. If you know you want to be a wife and a man clearly tells you that he has no interest in getting married, you need to move on. If being a forever girlfriend or "wifey" does not appeal to you, do not waste your time.

Men are simple. If he wants to be with you, he will claim you, that's it. He'll include you in his life, introduce you to his family, friends, etc. Men who are mature and ready to commit, go for what they want. They recognize you as the amazing woman you are, and know they want you in their lives. If a man is not ready to commit, don't take it personally. He is also a soul on his own path of evolution, having the experiences he needs to grow. Thank him for the lesson and move on.

One last note on "casual" sex before we go deeper into attracting our Most Compatible Soul Mate: I don't necessarily believe in sex being "casual." I believe it is an experience of healing with the potential to connect to spirit and manifest what we want in our lives. When we have sex with someone, we are exchanging energy with that person, which forges a connection. The more times you have sex with that person, the stronger the connection becomes. This is spiritual, but it is also chemical.

Our bodies release oxytocin, which is a bonding hormone, during lovemaking—the same hormone that is released when mothers breastfeed their babies. This chemical release sparks those "in love" feelings we begin to have. I have seen many women and men get "caught up" in relationships that started out as just "friends with benefits." But then it turns ugly when one party begins to "catch feelings" and tries to control the other. Things get messy as this push and pull toward the lover begins to ensue. You know you need to leave the other person alone, but you can't. The sexual energy has bonded you with that person.

Now, do I believe that you should "only" have sex inside of a committed relationship? No, I do not. Since my husband was the only person I was ever intimate with, after I left my marriage, I knew that I needed to have other experiences to know what I truly desired. I am very thankful for every experience I had from the wack and mundane, to the divinely orgasmic.

At this point in my life though, I am very careful as to whom I choose to "bond" with. If I have no desire to be connected to him, then I don't waste my time. If I desire commitment, then I do not need to be continuously sleeping with a man who does not. My actions need to be in alignment with my desires.

I'm calling in my Most Compatible Soul Mate, and I have no time for impostors. Now, of course, we all have needs and as a lover of sensuality, sex is like church to me, but at this point if I don't want to exchange spiritual energy and have my chemicals bonding to his, I'll just pleasure myself and call it a day.

You can decide where you are right now on the spectrum of "just wanting to explore, through dating" to "desiring a commitment with your Most Compatible Soul Mate." You know what your body and soul needs, but be honest and wise about what you can handle. Make sure your actions are in alignment with your true desires and don't put yourself in a situation where you're mistaking sex for a committed relationship. Communicate and be clear about what you want.

Also, if you're the one wanting sex without the commitment, then express that. I don't mean to paint a picture of women desperately clinging to men because of sex and a need for commitment. There have been men I've had around only for sex, whom I did not get caught up emotionally with whatsoever. But, because I know how much deeper and fulfilling connected sex is, the idea of that bores me. I've been on both sides, and honesty is key. I've witnessed far too many women get hurt and get caught up in confusing relationships with men. Be clear about you want and expect to receive it.

Calling in Your
Most Compatible Soul Mate

Now why do I say "most compatible"? In my opinion, one can have more than one soul mate. Soul Tie relationships are soul mate relationships. A soul mate is simply one who comes to connect you to your soul purpose and advance you on that mission. This is why you feel such an affinity toward these people. They reflect a latent energy in you that you need to develop. They are your mirror, as we discussed in chapter two.

So far I believe I have had three soul mate relationships. These individuals helped connect me to my soul purpose, but they are not my life partners. We came together for a reason and a season, and then once that mission was accomplished, it was time to move on. They helped me learn important lessons in preparation for the one who I believe will be my Most Compatible Soul Mate and life partner.

Goddesses, I want you to know I am just like you. I'm writing to you from a place of invoking my life partner. We are doing this together! I believe in my heart 100 percent that these practices that I am sharing with you will undoubtedly attract to me my Most Compatible Soul Mate. How do I know? It's simple. I create my life!

It is what I want, and I have faith that what I ask for, I will receive. He is coming, I know he is, and I excitedly await his unveiling! In the words of Shakti Gawain,

> *"This or something better manifests for me now in totally satisfying and harmonious ways for the highest good of all involved."*

And so it is!

As I prepare to receive my soul mate, I'd like to let you know what I'm doing to get ready. There are three steps I believe will lead us to a fulfilling relationship with our life partner.

Three Steps to Get Ready for Your Most Compatible Soul Mate

1. Love yourself.

2. Commit to your evolution.

3. Live your purpose.

Love Yourself

Chapter three was fully dedicated to teaching us the importance of loving ourselves. We explored practices that encouraged a juicy and pleasurable relationship with the woman in the mirror. I encourage you to continue to explore these techniques and cultivate a loving relationship with you. Model to others how they should treat you by the way you treat yourself. Be gentle and forgiving with yourself, even if you make a mistake. Realize you are worthy of real, true love and be the first person to give it to yourself.

A friend of mine has a self-love day once a week. She does not take any calls or make any appointments, but focuses that entire day on doing things that she wants to do. She makes a commitment to indulge in the essence of the love she has for herself.

This could be something you do, if not once a week, once a month. Take yourself to dinner or the movies. Get a pedicure or a manicure. Perhaps just sleep in. Do what you feel your body needs and answer to no one. Want a commitment? Commit to yourself first.

Commit to Your Evolution

If you want to attract an evolved mate, you must be fully invested in your growth and development. You're already on to a great start by reading this book. Continue to do the work that makes your soul reflect, evolve, and grow. Keep up with your daily sadhana practice. Perhaps take a meditation class or go on a yoga retreat, check out my Sensual Goddess Retreats.

Enroll in a coaching program to get more personal guidance (I am always available. Check out my programs and retreats at letgoletgoddess.com). Maybe volunteer at a shelter or mentor some youth. A lot of the time taking the attention from ourselves and giving it to someone else will quicken our evolution.

Deepen your spiritual practices. Perhaps become active in your church, temple, or whatever spiritual community you participate in. Ask your spirit, "What do you need most at this time to grow?" It will show you.

Live Your Purpose

I'd like to give a little more space to discuss step three of getting ready for your soul mate. The majority of this book is about steps one and two. But one of the most powerful things you can do to prepare for your life partner is to connect to your purpose.

Your purpose is your divine mission, it is why you chose to incarnate on this earth. Living in alignment with your purpose makes your life happy and fulfilling. When you are living a purpose-filled life, you open a wellspring of joy that nothing can replace. You move about the world with your special assignment, making a positive difference in the life of others while living your passion. Oprah said,

"There is no greater gift you can give or receive than to honor your calling. It's why you were born and how you become most alive."

Cultivate becoming truly alive! Thriving, not merely surviving, by living what you are called to do.

Sue Frederick wrote in her book, I See Your Soul Mate: An Intuitive's Guide to Finding and Keeping Love,

"Doing our true work will lead us to true love" (p. 59).

When you are doing something you truly love, you become the reflection of love. You give love, and love pours back into you; we attract what we are.

You come to your partner, not as a broken woman just floating through life without direction, but as a whole woman living in divine alignment. If you want to attract your Most Compatible Soul Mate, the one who is going to assist you in the evolution of your soul and achievement of your destiny, you must already be on the path. You must know who you are, so you can emit the proper frequency that calls in that resonate vibration to you.

As I said before, your Most Compatible Soul Mate shares a similar mission, your paths are complementary, and that's why you need each other so you can go further together than you ever could alone. Want to find your man? Find your purpose.

There are many women I coach who have no idea what their purpose is. They work at jobs they hate or that are unsatisfying. They feel lost and unconnected. Some women even fall to the false belief that they have no purpose. They think having a life purpose is only for the "special" few, such as Oprah or Dr. Martin Luther King. Untrue.

We ALL come to earth with a divine assignment. You might not be destined to entertain millions like Beyoncé or lead a world-changing movement like Gandhi, but you, my dear, have a purpose.

In Deepak Chopra's book, *The Seven Spiritual Laws of Success: A Practical Guide to the Fulfillment of Your Dreams,* he discusses powerful principles that when practiced will bring success in all aspects of life. The seventh principle in this book is "The Law of 'Dharma' or Purpose in Life." He writes,

> *"You have a talent that is unique in its expression, so unique that there's no one else alive on this planet that has that talent, or that expression of that talent. This means that there's one thing you can do . . . that is better than anyone else on this entire planet."*

Your unique and special talent is the key to unlocking your life purpose. Discover how to express your gift in a way that betters humankind, and you have your purpose. My purpose is to lead, teach, and inspire. For many years I worked as an educator in the public schools of New York City. I taught many subjects, such as reading, writing, and social studies. But my favorite subject was teaching middle school students theater arts.

What I loved most about my job was inspiring young people to step into their voice, creativity, and power. Seeing a quiet and shy seventh grader transform into a bold and bodacious character on stage was inspiring and life changing for both them and me. Now I teach and inspire women as a life coach. I use my gift of writing to create books and blogs that inspire women to heal and change their lives. While the container for my gifts and talents has changed, my purpose is still the same.

As you go through life, perhaps how you express your unique gifts and talents might change, but your core purpose will stay the same. What are your unique gifts and talents? Are you living a life that allows you to express that? What is your core purpose? If you are stuck in a dead end job, maybe it's time you find a different way to express your purpose or spend some time discovering what your purpose is. If you feel like you don't know your purpose, or would like to reignite it, I offer you the following Treasure Box Exercise as a way to connect to it.

This exercise is inspired by Paulo Coelho's book, *The Alchemist*. If you haven't read this book, then you need to get it and read it as soon as possible. It is a story about a shepherd boy's journey to find his treasure, and how he learns to trust his destiny. The treasure is really just a symbol for his purpose, and through his journey he discovers his unique gifts and talents and how to surrender to the wisdom and flow of the universe.

Coelho writes,

> *"Remember, wherever your heart is,*
> *there you will find your treasure."*

Search your heart for what makes you feel alive and connected, as Chopra says,

> *"the expression of that talent that*
> *takes you into a timeless awareness."*

What is in your treasure box?

Treasure Box Exercise

Make a list of things you like to do that makes you feel alive, connected, and joyful. What makes you light up and your soul sing? Try to list as many things as you can—from the profound to the mundane.

Look at your list. Some of these things might be hobbies, things you might not be interested in doing for other people or sharing with the world. Put a circle around those things that you enjoy that also connect to helping other people.

Now answer this question, from the things you circled, is there anything on the list that you love doing so much, that you'd do it for free? You get so much value and fulfillment from it, that that is the payment in itself?

Next, see if you can distill the one or two things you like doing so much that you would do it for free into a core purpose. What *exactly* are you doing? Are you healing, teaching, inspiring, informing, entertaining, beautifying, leading, etc.?

Last, now see if you can put it into a sentence, your core purpose plus the various outlets you use to express it. Here is mine:

"My core purpose is to lead, teach, and inspire through writing, leading workshops, and performing."

Write yours!

My core purpose is

_____

through

_____.

As I said, the avenue your purpose is expressed through might change, but your purpose remains the same. Allow your life to be fluid.

Ten years ago, when I first started teaching children, I never thought I'd wind up coaching women and writing self-help books. I thought perhaps one day I'd open up my own school or start a non-profit for youth arts. Fifteen years ago, I wanted to inspire people by performing as a stage actress.

Now all those things could very well happen one day, but my desires have been reshaped based on my life experiences. I am now building my own platform to teach and inspire, and the world is my stage! I'm sure even this vision will shift and morph with time. Always keep yourself open to the possibility to expand and change. Very often the vision we have for ourselves is smaller than what God has in store for us.

Purpose and Abundance

I want to share one last secret about living your purpose. Not only will answering your calling lead you to your Most Compatible Soul Mate, but it will also lead you to abundance. When you open to your purpose, you open for a divine vortex of energy to pour through you. This divine energy wants to be as effective as possible, so it conspires for your success. As you release resistance and give of your special gifts and talents, you will receive great reward in return. To quote Sue Frederick again,

"Our true work, the work we came here to do,
always DOES support us financially.
It's the only real path to abundance and success."

Release any fear-based thoughts you have that doing what you love will lead you to the poor house. Don't forsake your purpose because of trying to be "safe," you will end up stagnant and unsatisfied. I'm not saying, of course, to quit your job tomorrow and start your business of making beauty products (unless you believe that is what your spirit is saying is best for you right now). I am, however, saying don't let your gifts rot inside you.

Truth is, most people do not live a life connected to their purpose, they settle for being "safe" and die without getting to taste the real juiciness life has to offer. Get your juicy on, honor your calling.

Feminine Magnetism

Speaking of juicy, now that we've broken down the different kinds of men we might experience, discussed some guidelines for dating, and how to prepare for our Most Compatible Soul Mate, let's spice it up with some good ol' goddess juju! Let's turn on our feminine magnetism to attract the man of our dreams!

Before I give you the low-down on how to be a man magnet, I'd like to tell you a story about the power of feminine energy. In chapter three, I introduced you to Oshun, the Yoruba Goddess of Love. There is a famous pataki or fable about Oshun from the Ifá/Orisha tradition.

The story involves Oshun and the masculine god, Ogun. While there are various versions of the story, because it stems from an oral tradition, I give you a recount of the most essential points.

~~~~~

Long, long ago the orisha (divine deities) lived on earth. Oludumare (God) had given all the orisha dominion over different tasks in the world and various forces of nature. Each spirit had its own special abilities and magical powers. They helped humankind to evolve and create civilization.

One of the orisha, most responsible for the advancement of civilization, was Ogun, the god of iron. The people used the iron provided by Ogun to make tools to farm and create beautiful works of art. The ability to farm allowed the people to settle and establish communities. The creation of art brought about advancements in culture.

Now humans, being imperfect, began to squabble among themselves. They turned the iron tools given to them by Ogun into weapons of war. This made Ogun furious. Feeling unappreciated, he decided to retreat to the forest. With Ogun gone, civilization came to a halt. There was only misery and war.

The other orisha saw what was happening on earth and decided to intervene. One by one, they each went into the forest to try to persuade Ogun to come back so civilization could return and the suffering could stop. Oya, the orisha of the wind, sent a great tornado to blow around the forest, causing great destruction, but Ogun refused. Shango, the orisha of fire and lightning, made bolts of lightning set fire to the earth, all around Ogun's forest, but Ogun ignored it. Each orisha, in their own ways, tried to convince Ogun to return, but he still refused.

The orisha wondered what they should do. If Ogun did not return, then civilization would forever be destroyed. Finally, Oshun, the orisha of beauty and love, said, "Let me try."

Oshun went to the forest in her most elegant, sheer dress. Once in the forest, she placed herself where she knew Ogun would see her. There she disrobed and began pouring honey, her favorite food, all over her body. She then began dancing sweetly and sensually. Ogun tried to ignore Oshun, but he was captivated. The sound of her voice was like the ringing of bells, and her movements were like the river.

Oshun, knowing Ogun was watching her, began to dance through the forest. Ogun could not help but follow her. Oshun played hide and seek with the trees, leading Ogun farther and farther away from where he had retreated. She allowed him, once, to get close enough to almost catch her, and she smeared some honey on his lips. After that it was over, Ogun was hers.

Before Ogun knew it, he was out of the forest and back in the village. By this time, he was begging to be with Oshun. Oshun agreed that she would be with him on one condition, that he returned to help humankind and never retreat again. Ogun, of course, agreed. Civilization returned to the earth and Oshun showered Ogun with her love.

~~~~~

This ancient myth illustrates the power of sweetness over force and brutality. Oshun was able to save Ogun and therefore save the world. She conquered the god of iron and war, not with harshness but with gentleness. In her special way she was able to do what no other god could do. Oshun embodies the magical ability that all women have to magnetize and attract through softness and sweet femininity.

Feminine Energy and Masculine Energy

Many have heard of the concept "men are from Mars, and women are from Venus." This idea is rooted in the basic concept that men and women are inherently different. Not just different physically, though that is definitely true, but also different energetically. In the Taoist tradition, men are associated with yang energy and women with yin energy. We spoke of this briefly in chapter two, but let's break it down some more.

All of creation is made from the intermingling of two forces, yin and yang. Yin translates to mean shadow, and yang means light. Yin is characterized to be slow, soft, yielding, diffuse, cold, wet, and passive. It is associated with water, earth, the Moon, femininity, and nighttime. Yang, by contrast, is fast, hard, solid, focused, hot, dry, and aggressive. It is associated with fire, the sky, the Sun, masculinity, and daytime.

Understand, these forces are not oppositional forces that are struggling against one another. In reality, there is only ONE energy, this original energy had to split into yin and yang, or masculine and feminine, in order for creation to happen. These forces are complementary and interdependent on each other—both are needed for life to manifest. Yin and yang are indispensable dualities of the same one self.

Coming from this divine original energy, we are polarized into male or female bodies. The attraction we have for each other, as men and women, comes from a desire to achieve balance. When we mate with our partners, we, as women, feed the feminine essence within man, and they feed the masculine within us (within yang there is always yin, and within yin there is always yang).

The drive that we have to achieve partnership, to relate, fall in love, and have sex comes from a desire to resolve the male/female polarity split of the original self. Love holds a neutral place where our yin and yang can become balanced. This is why we feel so wonderful and happy when in love; our partner helps us to achieve divine completeness.

While, of course, we need to be happy and whole as an individual, once that is achieved it is time to unite with a partner to catapult us to the next level. Women need men, and men need women, point blank. Yin and yang must feed and balance each other.

The story of Oshun and Ogun illustrates that so well. The sacred masculine energy of Ogun needed the sweet feminine essence of Oshun to draw him out of seclusion, and help him to step back into his power. Without the support of the yin, the masculine will exhaust itself. Without the yang, the yin will become stagnant and nonproductive.

So if you're one of those women walking around saying, "I don't need a man." Then trust and believe you will remain single and without a man. In order for us to attract our Most Compatible Soul Mate, we have to allow ourselves to tap into our feminine energy and become vulnerable.

After my divorce, I too walked around saying, "I don't need a man." Saying this made me feel "strong," like I could do it all on my own, and it validated a belief in my own power, or, so I thought. What it really did was put up walls to hide my true feelings. It prevented me from really connecting to the men I dated.

When a woman says, "I don't need a man," she is lying. What she is really saying is, "I've been hurt in the past and I'm scared of being hurt again, so I'm hiding my heart to protect myself." She is walking around in a broken masculine shell. What she is really craving is to be treated gently with care, so she can melt into her feminine essence.

So, if you want to bring in your Most Compatible Soul Mate you must realize, yes, you do need a man! You need to become vulnerable and radiate the sweet feminine energy that your masculine man desperately needs. A lot of women cringe when they hear the words "soft" and "vulnerable." They choke when they think about being submissive to a man, because they equate femininity with weakness.

As Oshun so clearly illustrates, gentleness and feminine energy can conquer the toughest of warriors. If you think of water, the element that is linked to yin, it is arguably the most powerful element on this planet and certainly the most abundant, making up 70 percent of the earth. As Lao Tzu intuited,

"Nothing is softer or more flexible than water,
yet nothing can resist it."

There is also a Yoruba saying that goes,

"No one is an enemy to water."

It is water that extinguishes fire. Water will gently wear away at hard substances, drip by drip, causing them to eventually fall apart. Water also has the ability to morph into all states of matter—liquid, solid, and gas. Women are like water. Oshun is the goddess of the river. What can stop a flowing river? Do not underestimate the power of feminine energy—there is nothing weak about it!

To help us tap into our feminine energy, I am going to share with you a Love Goddess Bath inspired by Oshun. If you are looking to unleash your yin, attract dates or your life partner, do this bath every Friday for five weeks, then take a break. You can also do it five nights in a row. You can repeat as long as you need the cycle of five baths (five is Oshun's sacred number).

Love Goddess Exercise #1
Sweet Love Goddess Bath

Tools

- ✓ yellow flowers
- ✓ ½ gallon cow's milk
- ✓ 1 quart goats milk
- ✓ ½ cup of cinnamon
- ✓ ½ cup of brown sugar
- ✓ 1 cup of honey
- ✓ 1 small bottle of Florida water (find in grocery store, botanica or online)
- ✓ 1 cup of white wine
- ✓ 5 drops sandalwood oil or sweet perfume
- ✓ sandalwood incense
- ✓ 7 day yellow candle

Preparation: Gather your ingredients. While it might look like these items could help you bake a cake, what they do is energetically call the spirit of femininity, love, and attraction to your life. Before running the bath, take a quick shower to clean your body. Then run the water nice and hot for your bath.

Bath Ritual

When the bath is half full, you can begin adding in the ingredients.

As you add each ingredient, say a prayer asking that the spiritual qualities of love and magnetism of each be released into the water. Ask Oshun to bless you with the magical powers of feminine energy and bring love into your life (this includes self-love).

Be sure to taste the honey before you pour it into the bath, asking that your words and essence be sweet to attract pleasant, loving experiences to you.

Before you pour the wine into the water, pour a glass for yourself and take some sips while relaxing in the bath.

Sit inside the bath for at least 30 minutes. It should feel amazing and luxurious. Massage your body, the milk should feel lovely on your skin. Say prayers and affirmations. Visualize what you want in a relationship.

Once you are finished soaking, get out of the tub and allow yourself to air dry. Do not towel the energy off or rinse off with plain water. You want the essence of the bath to remain on your body.

Dress in light- or white-colored clothing. Do a meditation or journal and go to bed. The next day, be sure to wear light-colored clothing. If you really want to tap into Oshun, wear her color—yellow. Feel free to beautify yourself with jewelry, a little makeup, pretty clothes, a flower in your hair, etc.

As you go throughout your day, try to be sweet, and don't get into an argument with anyone. Focus on being one with your soft feminine energy.

Notice what happens, and how you feel. Feel free to flirt and give someone your number, if you attract someone you want to get to know better.

The Power of Sweet Femininity

Enjoy playing with your feminine energy! Being a woman is so powerful; we get to be the iron fist in a soft velvet glove.

Practice getting your way through being sweet as opposed to being forceful, force will drive a man away, being sweet like honey will attract him. Allow yourself to receive from a man. Men love to feel needed and helpful, welcome his assistance. This applies to all men. Practice with the men you meet everywhere, at the grocery store checkout, customer assistants, the bus driver, etc. See how men respond when you radiate sweetness, and see how easily you get what you want. Smile more, and let the joy you have within radiate out to the world.

When dating, if he asks you out, let him pay for dinner. Allow him to open the door for you, take out the trash, etc. Let him step into his role of the masculine energy that needs to lead, provide, and protect. This does not mean you're a doormat or you let him lead you down a dark hole of ruin. Above all, men want to please you, so be please-able and encouraging. Watch him go to any lengths to put a smile on your face, and enjoy the quiet power you wield!

As you are working on attracting love, be careful about listening to songs about heartbreak, cheating, lying men, etc. We don't often realize how these messages get embedded into our subconscious and program our beliefs about love.

If you have a girlfriend who has a lot of man problems, be careful of how much time you spend with her. You don't want to pick up her troubled energy. Send her light and love, but don't take on her issues. She must learn, just as you are. Give her a copy of my book, if she's open to learning.

Also don' t take advice from women who are bitter, heartbroken, and pessimistic. Sometimes when others see you wanting a partner, they proceed to piss on your parade by saying how there aren't any good men around. Shield yourself from their venom. Watch your words and what you say, speak life into your love life. Above all, allow yourself to feel safe enough to know it's fine to be a smart, beautiful, evolved, independent woman who still needs a man and is comfortable in her soft feminine energy. If you never open to love, you never will receive it.

Affirmations to change your thoughts about love:

I open myself to give and receive love.

I am a man magnet!
I easily attract compatible men who
love taking me out on dates.

I am connected to my soft, feminine essence and
easily magnetize what I want to me.

The love and joy I have within me overflows
out into the world, I receive love and joy in return.

I am already deeply connected to my
Most Compatible Soul Mate.
We will meet at the perfect place and at the perfect time.

Ask and Receive!

Now that we have turned on our magnetism and feminine energy, let's get clear about what we want and ask the universe to deliver. Do you know what you want in a man? So many women I coach do not have a clear picture of what they're trying to attract. I had to get married and divorced to figure out what I wanted in a man. With every man I date, the picture becomes clearer.

Make a list of what you want in a man. Write everything that you want, don't limit yourself. Think about the inner qualities that are important to you, which you feel would make a lasting partnership. You can also include physical characteristics, habits, and lifestyle. Try to get as clear as possible. I suggest making a list of 15–20 things. Once you have that overall list, I want to you to go through it and find five things you most want your partner to have that are nonnegotiable. Really think about those deep essential qualities that are important to you. Here is an example:

5 Essential Qualities

1. Kindhearted

2. Living his purpose

3. Spiritual

4. Fun

5. Financially secure

Once you have these essential five qualities, I want you to take each one and write a reflection on them. Are you actively cultivating these qualities in your own life? Write about where you are landing with each quality and how you can be more of it. There are women who want a financially secure man but have no financial stability themselves. We attract what we are. So if you want a man who has these qualities, nurture them in yourself.

You can place your entire list on your altar. Ask spirit to bring you someone who is a reflection of what you want or far greater. Most of the times we get far greater.

I'd like to share with you a meditation and ritual to plant your desire for your life partner into the womb of the universe. You can do this meditation every night, or when you feel inclined to call in your Most Compatible Soul Mate. It is a powerful meditation, so use it wisely. If you're not ready for your life partner, then don't call him yet.

Love Goddess Exercise #2
Most Compatible Soul Mate Meditation

Tools: Your imagination and loving presence

Preparation: Relax, put on some soothing music and wear loose, comfortable clothing.

Meditation: Imagine you are sitting in a sacred forest, wearing a white dress. It is a beautiful, sunny day, you hear the birds singing, the sun is shining, and everything seems to be illuminated. You have come here to meet your beloved. You know he is coming, and you are waiting. You close your eyes to call him silently with your energy.

Visualize yourself breathing deeply, as a white light begins to shine from your belly. This light shines brightly from your belly and moves up your body and out of your head. See the light leaving the forest, shining, and moving throughout the world, seeking the resonate vibration that matches yours, the light of your perfect partner.

Your light finds your perfect partner wherever he is. See your partner; he is also dressed in white. He has a bright light shining from his belly. See your lights mesh together as one and, as they do, both your lights begin to draw him to you. See the light pull your Most Compatible Soul Mate to you, until he is in the forest walking toward you.

Stand before your perfect partner and allow him to embrace you. Hear him tell you how much he loves you and how he is seeking you too. He assures you that at the perfect place and the perfect time, you will meet each other. Tell him how much you love him and that you can't wait to meet him.

Hug your perfect partner, feel your energies melt into the other and become one. Allow yourself to feel gratitude for having found each other. After a while, let him go. See him going back to wherever he is, know that his light is connected to you, and your light is connected to him. Trust the universe to deliver him to you in divine timing.

Tips for the Meditation

The more you do it, the stronger connection you will feel. When I do this meditation, I try not to see a specific person. I focus more on how he feels, in order to not limit myself so I can be open to whomever he might be. Surrender your desire, and believe you will have what you ask for!

Love Goddess Exercise #3
Sacred Oshun Offering

This final ritual I offer you comes from the Orisha tradition. It is an offering to the goddess of love, Oshun. This ritual is powerful and will yield results, so I strongly advise you to take it seriously. In my work with Oshun, she always comes and gives me what is best for me at the time. Though she is sweet and full of love, her energy is not to be trifled with. She is to be approached with reverence and respect.

In this ritual, you are going to go to the waters of Oshun and pray to attract your Most Compatible Soul Mate. You can also go to her with issues you have in your life, including any dealing with feminine and reproductive problems, fertility, money, creativity, etc. These are her areas of expertise. You need to find a moving body of "sweet" water—no oceans—that is a different energy. Rivers are best, moving lake waters are also fine.

Tools: The river, a pumpkin (there many types, I like to use the kabocha "squash." Lots of Caribbean dishes use this and call it pumpkin), honey, five coins, a knife, pen and paper.

Preparation: Wear a long skirt or wrap some cloth around your pants, if it's cold. Oshun is a feminine energy and skirts allow our feminine energy to flow.

Ritual

You are going to write a letter to Oshun, praying for the things you'd like to see in your life. I usually limit my asking to five things, as that is her number. If you want your life partner, tell her what you are looking for. You always want to start your letter with gratitude for what you have already. Ask her to help you be as sweet as honey, so you might attract what you need in your life—ask her to sweeten your life.

Once you have your letter, you are going to take the pumpkin, the letter, knife, coins, and honey to the river. If you like, you can write the letter at the river. I find it relaxing to sit by the side of the water as I write my prayers.

After you finish your letter, you are going to cut a circle around the stem of the pumpkin so you can open it up without destroying it. Pumpkins are sacred to Oshun and represent wealth and fertility; they are symbolic of the womb.

You might have to work the knife around a few times, ask the pumpkin for permission to open it, and it should pop open like a bottle top. Place the letter and five coins inside the pumpkin. Open the honey, taste it to sweeten yourself, and then pour it inside the pumpkin on top of your letter and the coins. Place the top back on the pumpkin—it should fit like a puzzle piece.

Walk down to the river's edge and say your prayer to Oshun. Tell her what you've brought her and what you desire. Ask for her assistance and thank her for hearing your prayers.

Once you are done, place the pumpkin in the water. Turn around without looking back and walk away from the river.

A Note on This Love Goddess Assignment: You should see results quite soon. If you are not ready for your Most Compatible Soul Mate, Oshun will bring you the lessons you need to learn as a preparation for your life partner. Men love Oshun's sweet energy, so you might see an increase in suitors. If you have men around you who are not good for you, you might also see them blocked from you and start to fall away. Accept whatever happens as being in alignment with what's best for you.

As with anything you pray and ask for, release it and have no attachment to the results. Trust that you will receive what you have asked for, but surrender the "how" and "when." Every time that I have prayed for something or "someone" and not received what I wanted, it has always been revealed to me later why it was not for my best interest or I received something better. Surrender is the key word!

I will seal this chapter with a quote from *The Alchemist*. Fatima, the love of the shepherd boy, tells him these words,

*"I love you because the
entire universe conspired to help me find you."*

Trust in your personal legend, and trust that life is conspiring for your highest good. Open your heart and receive all you desire. And so it is!

Concluding Thoughts

The journey to heal from heartbreak and open to new love is one of the most challenging but rewarding paths we can go on. Ultimately, it is a journey to the self, our true self. Our lovers are our greatest lessons and highest spiritual curriculum. If you want to grow and see your "shit," fall in love (I would also add have children to that). Approach this whole thing as an adventure; however, you are the "shero" of your own story. You are not looking for a prince to come "save" you—you are working to save yourself.

Don't put your wholeness or happiness on hold until you meet the perfect partner either. If you do, you will not attract the right one to you. You will attract your reflection, another person looking for fulfillment through relationships. Another possibility is that you will meet someone who embodies what you want, but you will be terrified and run, or sabotage the relationship with your unresolved issues.

Many women predicate their happiness on being in a relationship. But having or not having a partner should not affect your inner joy. Do not be afraid to be by yourself! I know many women who are constantly in and out of relationships with men, spending no significant period of time reflecting by themselves. If you are one of the women who have always been in a relationship in some shape or form, I really encourage you to spend time alone.

During this time, focus on your healing and delve into getting to know who you are outside of being in a relationship with a man. Many people, but women especially, treat being single as some sign of failure, especially after a certain age. It does not matter how damaged or fractured you are, somehow if you have a "man," then you are better than women who don't. This is a harmful fallacy as it perpetuates notions of incompleteness outside of a romantic partner and the continuous cycle of pathological intimate connections.

Matchmaker Paul Carrick Brunson in his book *It's Complicated (But It Doesn't Have to Be): A Modern Guide to Finding and Keeping Love* talks about people treating being single as some "horrid disease." Society through cliché Hollywood films, books, and magazines pumps fantasies into the minds of people that finding "the one" will solve everything wrong in their lives. Brunson writes,

"So marriage isn't to be treated as a fluffy never-ending high of candy-coated kisses and mind-blowing 'honeymoon' sex, nor is marriage to be treated as the end all, be all, defining factor in your long-term happiness that without it you will be less of a person" (p. 13).

There are people in relationships who are completely miserable, and people who are single and totally blissed out. As a life coach, I counsel people who are unhappy, because they want to be in a relationship. I also counsel people who have great partners and are *still* unhappy.

You must be happy with *You*! Erase the notion that being single somehow makes you less than someone who is married or in a relationship. Truthfully, how many happily married people do you know? For those who are unhappy, marriage isn't the problem, however, they are. As a single person, you have the opportunity to fully create the kind of relationship you want, but that relationship begins with you.

In all things, be gentle with yourself. Sometimes, you will "fall" down, you will forget how powerful you are, you will sell yourself short, and you will want to give up. You might see other people who are not working as hard as you, who are in seemingly happy relationships. Don't be jealous, that blocks your blessings. Wish them well and remember that everything is not always what it seems. Keep focusing on your inner work and growth. Enjoy your life exactly as it is so you can attract more joy, love, and abundance.

Above all, don't give up. You are in a sacred dance to fall more in love with you and share your purpose with the planet. As you do, the world will fall in love with you too. In the midst of your dance, there might arrive a masculine reflection ready to bust a move with you. When he comes, welcome him, and keep the party going. Pour him a glass of champagne, and give him the lap dance of his life!

With tremendous gratitude and adoration for ALL the work you have done, I wish you well on the path to manifesting your deepest desires and the love you deserve.

May you live happy and healed!

Goddess Blessings,

Lady Shepsa Jones

References

Brunson, Paul Carrick. *It's Complicated (But It Doesn't Have to Be): A Modern Guide to Finding and Keeping Love.* (Gotham, 2012).

Chopra, Deepak. The Seven Spiritual Laws of Success: A Practical Guide to the Fulfillment of Your Dreams. (New World Library, 1004).

Coelho, Paulo. *The Alchemist.* (HarperOne, 1993).

Frederick, Sue. I See Your Soul Mate: An Intuitive's Guide to Finding and Keeping Love. (St. Martin's Press, 2012).

Richardson, Diana. *Tantric Orgasm for Women.* (Destiny Books, 2004).

Singer, Sydney Ross and Soma Grismaijer. *Dressed to Kill: The Link between Breast Cancer and Bras.* (ISCD Press, 2002).

Some, Sobonfu E. Welcoming Spirit Home: Ancient African Teachings to Celebrate Children and Community. (New World Library, 1999).

About the Author

Lady Shepsa Jones is a writer, teacher, life coach, mother, and "juju woman"—one who taps into her magical powers for healing and manifestation. A shy girl, she started writing at a young age to express her emotions. Recognized for her talents early on, she won many awards, including Presidential Scholar in the Arts, National Foundation for Advancements in the Arts Award, and was a first-place winner in the Philadelphia Young Playwrights Contest.

As she grew older, her love of the arts expanded into performance and acting. She holds a BFA with honors in drama from New York University, where she also double majored in Africana studies. As an adult, she has spent more than ten years studying the spiritual sciences of the African Diaspora, along with the Taoist and Tantric traditions.

Through the study of sacred sexuality, Shepsa has reconnected to the goddess within her and aims to assist other women in experiencing the healing and freedom of their sensual selves. In 2012, she published a poetry book called *The Goddess Pages: Honey, Full Moons and Daggers*.

She is also a certified i2Tantra practitioner with JujuMama LLC and a certified yoga teacher. She was published in *Corset's Magazine's* "Sacred Sex" issue and a featured blogger on *My Tiny Secrets*. Shepsa has also led workshops at many conferences and events for women.

Always evolving, Shepsa is now leading women in healing circles, sacred sexuality workshops, group coaching programs, and retreats.

Connect with Me

Thank you for reading this book. If you'd like to leave a review about this book on Amazon, please do!

Let's stay in touch!

Website

http://letgoletgoddess.com/

Facebook

https://www.facebook.com/LetGoLetGoddess

Twitter

https://twitter.com/ladyshepsa

YouTube

Let Go Let Goddess

Instagram

@letgoletgoddess

www.ingramcontent.com/pod-product-compliance
Lightning Source LLC
Chambersburg PA
CBHW072150090426
42740CB00012B/2206